THE CAMINO LETTERS

The Camino Letters

26 Tasks on the Way to Finisterre

JULIE KIRKPATRICK

PYXIS PRESS

MILLBROOK

Library and Archives Canada Cataloguing in Publication

Kirkpatrick, Julie, 1968– .
    The Camino letters : 26 tasks on the way to Finisterre / Julie Kirkpatrick.

ISBN 978-0-9865134-0-4 (bound).—ISBN 978-0-9865134-1-1 (pbk.)

    1. Kirkpatrick, Julie, 1968–   —Travel—Spain—Santiago de Compostela.
2. Santiago de Compostela (Spain).   3. Spain, Northern—Description and travel.
I. Title.

DP402.S23K57 2010   914.6'11   C2010-903693-X

16 15 14 13 12 11 10   2 3 4 5 6 7 8 9

Pyxis Press, Post Office Box 382, Millbrook, Ontario, Canada. L0A 1G0
www.pyxispress.com
www.thecaminoletters.com

Pyxis Press is distributed in North America by
Broadview Press, Post Office Box 1243, Peterborough, Ontario, Canada. K9J 7H5
Phone: (705) 743-8990
Fax: (705) 743-8353
E-mail: customerservice@broadviewpress.com
www.broadviewpress.com

Printed in the United States of America

Preface

ON A WHIM, IN THE summer of 2009, I decided to walk the Camino de Santiago with my seventeen-year-old daughter. The only preparation that I made for the trip was to request twenty-six tasks from twenty-six friends — one for me to complete each day while I walked.

I had almost no idea where the Camino was. And I definitely did not set out on a pilgrimage, although I knew that this was an ancient pilgrimage route. In my mind, I was simply going on a long walk with my daughter, and for this purpose I closed my law practice for a month and left my life behind.

The very real experience of pilgrimage came to me only while walking. The act of putting one foot in front of the other, day after day, with only my tasks to answer to, led me on an interior journey that I was not prepared for and was not expecting.

The chapters in this book are the letters I wrote on the Camino, simply written to my friends in answer to my tasks. They were sent individually to each taskmaster, and then later read aloud in sequence to my father before he died in December, 2009.

Many of my twenty-six taskmasters have not met each other. This odd connection to me may be the only thing that they share in common. I am deeply grateful to all twenty-six, and I offer this volume, a documented quest of spirit by a very reluctant and humbled pilgrim, as my small gift in return.

I am also grateful to my children, who remain my greatest teachers, particularly on the subject of forgiveness; to my husband, who is my everlasting rock; to Miss Malakai, for sticking with me all the way to Finisterre; and to my father for taking me with him to the place of my greatest fear and for showing me the beauty and the pain and the power of leaving the cocoon.

Millbrook, January 23, 2010

Introduction

JUNE 13, 2009

I NEED TO ASK YOU A favour. I am leaving in two weeks for Spain and plan to spend at least twenty-six days in July walking the Camino pilgrimage route.

I will need something to focus on, I think, and so I have decided to play a little game with myself. What I need from you is a task to take with me: anything — physical, mental, emotional, spiritual. I'll need the details by June 21.

I am going to have twenty-six things to do or think about, from twenty-six people. You are one. :-)
jk

JUNE 23, 2009

Julie:

I HAVE DECIDED TO CHANGE MY trip challenge for you. Forget recitation of as many countries of the world as you can, how very mundane. No, the challenge is this: Write the first chapter of your book, in your head if you like.
/JJ

FINISTERRE, JULY 25, 2009

Dear Jim:

I AM WRITING THIS "FIRST CHAPTER" as a direct consequence of your email, simply for you. I am sitting at Finisterre, *Terra Finis*, the end of the world where the sun meets the water. I have waited until today to write to you in response to your task because this is, of course, the end of my Camino travels and the near completion of twenty-six individual tasks requested on a whim and given to me by twenty-six very dear friends.

People say many things about the Camino and, after a month of walking, I think I heard most of it along the way from people who had researched their adventure far more thoroughly than I did. They say that tears are poured into the stones of the Camino. There is much talk and metaphor about "letting go" of "stuff" along the way. They say that you will meet the people you need to meet on the Camino. This is what they say. At the beginning, I often wondered if I was the only one who didn't know what it was that I was supposed to be experiencing here. It is a pilgrimage route, after all. But I did not come here to be a pilgrim, as in "To Be a Pilgrim" in the hymn books.

In the beginning, I thought that people were talking about the walk as "my Camino" in an inauthentic and self-aggrandizing way. The Camino is alive, they say. Beyond the Christian pilgrims, reaching far back to the Celts, people say that the Camino is energetically and astrologically in sync with the power of the whole universe. They say that specific points on the Camino mirror the chakras in the body, and these are where the Templars built their churches. It all seemed very soft and sentimental: "woo woo," according to my children. I considered it quite differently than this. I was going to start walking, get in shape, and do my little tasks to keep my mind occupied. That was pretty much it. A very lawyerly approach, don't you think?

In fact, I knew next to nothing about the Camino. I was so panicked and jittery about getting everything done before I left that I couldn't even open the books in the travel section at the bookstore. I had too many other things on my mind. All I knew before getting here was that it was a pilgrimage route somewhere in Spain for Celts and Catholics, neither of which I am. And I knew about Oliver Schroer, the Canadian violinist who had played in churches along the Camino, recording his beautiful improvised music as he went. My friend Brian gave me Schroer's CD a long time ago which, very true to form, I took years to return. I listened to it only once before I left Canada. But now I have listened to Schroer on the plane, on the train, while going to sleep on late evenings in my bed to drown out the snoring around me, and on the bus to Finisterre. I feel this music like I have not felt any other. I feel the pain and the sadness and the fear and the thanksgiving, and I was so very lucky to have been able to carry it with me.

The churches that Oliver Schroer played in were opened to him only by chance or by stealth as he walked through the many towns and villages along the way. He did not bring music and he did not compose in advance. He simply played in sacred spaces and recorded himself with a very simple device. I have written letters each day in response to my various tasks, and I suppose, in its way, it is the same thing. I have recorded myself along this route with a very simple device — my pen and my heart. *Par coeur*, as my friend Dominic would and did instruct.

Many of the churches on the Camino are built on the vestiges of other, older things. For a Canadian, the idea of something being older, hidden but palpable, in the foundations of a magnificent twelfth-century Romanesque church, is unfathomable. But it is true. Villages still stand where entire populations were wiped out by plague. You were the one who told me that it was thought, at the time, that the witches were to blame, so all of the black cats were killed, leaving the rat population to multiply and spread the disease. Why is it that the witches were always to blame?

Some say that the Camino follows the old Celtic route, beginning I don't know where. My guess would be at Skellig Michael in Ireland, said to be the fount of the St. Michael Ley, if you believe that sort of thing, which I don't know if I do. The Celtic route predated Santiago by a millennium, and Finisterre is at the end, where the sun meets the land meets the water – the home of the Sun god. The cathedral at Santiago, three days before Finisterre, holds the relics of St. James and is the end of the Catholic route. In 1214, St. Francis of Assisi completed the pilgrimage along the north coast, following the Camino Norte and the Camino Primitivo from San Salvador de Oviedo to Santiago. The Roman road and medieval bridges remain – it was a Roman trade route – following *la voje ladee* (the Milky Way) to Finis Terra. Here, the Druids worshipped father Dis at the end of the world.

In the end, I know for certain that there is something to all of it – this universal hunger and the attempts to describe the indescribable – hidden, yet palpable and resting on the foundations of older things. Pilgrimage is common to all religion: Christian, Hindu, Buddhist, Muslim, pagan. It is part of a universal yearning for the soul, the higher self, the immeasurable, and the infinite.

I did not set out on a pilgrimage. I was (and kept myself) too busy to ever consider it, frankly. The day before I left, my husband kindly suggested that we walk twenty or so kilometres to Port Hope, perhaps with me carrying my pack, and my response to him was, sincerely: "Are you crazy? Why would I want to do that?" On the flight from Toronto to Paris, I sat next to a young Iranian doctoral student from the University of Toronto. She was flying to France to hike through the Pyrenees. In my journal that I kept, I made a note of this: "Pyrenees — where is that?"

The answer, as I would soon discover, is that the Pyrenees are the mountains over which I would walk on the first day from St. Jean Pied de Port to Roncesvalles, places now so familiar but up till then so foreign. I was an unprepared and reluctant pilgrim. I had no clue.

I can yearn with the best of them, given the time, but this month that I have spent on the Camino was definitely not part of my personal bargain with the universe. My deal with the universe, to be brutally honest (and of course, Jim, you know all of this already), comes from my own little history. My life's journey is no more difficult and painful than most others, and far, far less so than the majority of the inhabitants of this planet — but still it's mine, and I hold it very close:

Dear Universe:
Let me live until my children are grown. And don't let me lose my mind. I can be blind, that's okay. But please don't let what happened to my beautiful mother happen to me. Or if I must suffer a similar illness and death, then let me have a lawyer friend, like Sue maybe, who will make them legalize euthanasia. That's all. I'll be good and I won't be selfish and I'll work really, really hard until then. That's it. Thanks.

This was my secret deal with whatever is out there in the Universe. I have never said this out loud in one piece. Why would I? These things are to be kept silent and hidden. Suck it up. Carry on. And for God's sake, don't cry.

And yet it's palpable, isn't it? The fear and the pain that we carry, in fact carries us. It has a sense and a smell that arrives long before we do. And it lingers long after we are gone.

Regardless of all of that, after walking almost 600 kilometres, approximately 300 of which I walked completely alone, I can say it out loud. I have said it out loud. And it would appear that perhaps my deal with the Universe is not my deal to make. In fact, there is no deal. It is what it is. One foot in front of the other. Long live the Queen. Whatever. Amen. That, in a nutshell, is my Camino.

I did not expect this. But nor did I expect the tasks that I received in response to my silly email. I did not expect to be taken seriously by my friends, and I did not expect to be given tasks with heart and soul in mind. These tasks have provided me with a crutch on which to rest my thoughts as I walked, and an umbrella for my tears as they fell. I have clung to my tasks with all of my soul, silly as that might sound when I say it out loud.

My very last task came to me on the day before I left, from my friend Felice who drove it out to Millbrook with specific instructions not to open it until I was on the plane. Felice came back the next day, before we left for the airport, to deliver her mother's rosary for me to carry. Her mother had died when Felice was pregnant with her first child. I remember having a long conversation with Felice about the deaths of our mothers, in a park in Peterborough, before I knew her well. In my house, Felice's beautiful and kind mother is a woman of some legend, since as a child my husband knew both of them. To be so entrusted with Felice's mother's rosary was almost too much to bear. It was then that I knew that if I was going to be true to what I had received from my friends, I was going to have to do some very hard slogging.

Walking the Camino in this way, with my tasks in hand, has been the most difficult thing I have ever had to do. And it quickly became something I had to do, without that being my intention. I have tried not to share too much with people I meet about who I think I am. I have tried to "be" more than a lawyer, and have indeed been more whole and full and alive than I had remembered being possible. I have been forced, and have forced myself, to move beyond all of those things that I think I am: small, unhealthy, a wife, a mother, a lawyer, and a daughter. Here, writing to you from Finisterre, I can say to you that I have remembered that I am far more than all of those things. I can't believe I'm actually writing that; it's so simple. Doesn't it sound so simple? I wonder why I couldn't have figured that out 600 kilometres and a whole ocean ago.

Perhaps all of the research and all of the preparation that people do before a big trip is really of no assistance on the Camino. Perhaps the essence of pilgrimage is not in the preparation, but in the very simple act of putting one foot in front of the other, step after step, day after day, week after week, regardless of the starting intention. It is also a matter of consciously going in the same direction as other people, past and present, on the same path. Messy, snoring people who keep me up at night. Beautiful, strong people who pass me with their sure-footed saunter. All of the people on the Camino are all walking, and all going the same way. It's the same as life itself really — forward in life unto death, or as my dad says often and so very wisely: "You just have to put one foot in front of the other until you fall off the cliff."

BECAUSE OF MY TASKS, I have cried more in a month than I have in all my forty years, and I have been forced to think and think and mourn and pound my anger into the hard, cracked clay earth with my walking poles up endless, despised mountains. I have also been forced immediately (by the next day's task) to set myself completely aside and be attentive to others, in Spanish no less. I have fought with, been abandoned by, and made up with my teenaged daughter many, many times. I have been grateful for the time away from her and I have been happy to find her again. I have learned to stand alone in the face of her, the fiercest critic of my Camino – and to love her with all my soul, whether she sees it immediately or not.

I have struggled with the weight of my pack and my flabby thighs, and not even two weeks later felt utterly triumphant striding up mountains and beating the "Basque dudes" to the top. My endurance and my strength have astounded me. My freedom in my confused and temperamental physical body is a cause for celebration. On the second day, I danced with butterflies. On the fourth day, I walked half-blind and I was not afraid. On the eleventh day, I played my flute for the grasshoppers. I must not forget this.

I have made many friends, some of whom I have never spoken to in a common language. I tried to understand witch-burnings in Spanish, Italian, French, and Basque. I have expressed myself fully, wholly, with my face, my hands, and all that I am.

I was told repeatedly in at least five languages in different places, by different people, that fear and love are the only two emotions in life. I found rock art saying the same thing. You find what you need on the Camino, they say – and they, whoever they are, may well be right. I could walk around the whole world; I am that strong. I am not afraid. I am full of love.

My friend Suzan once told me that she had never seen anyone sweep out the corners like me, and I suppose there is some truth in that. I've never turned that ability on myself until now, but that is where my tasks have led me. And with everything else, although

I do blather on a fair bit about it all, the real stuff, the deeper stuff, has been very quiet.

In the end, only I truly understand the magic of my tasks, and that's the whole point. What I have done here is not research – it is me. I've just been slogging through my own little life. You tasked me with writing the first chapter of a book, and I have done so. This is it. You think that I have a talent that should not be wasted on pleadings and affidavits – thank you so much for telling me that. You confirmed in me something that I have always known, and I am so grateful for being unleashed and un-locked. I was free to write my letters from my heart, *par coeur*, and I did. Dear Jim: Thank you.

And in the end, when you read all of the letters, I think you will see that I have discovered something very simple. I love my-self for being the pure spirit of light that I am, and I love my life for being the pure light that it is. And I really mean it. I said it out loud. That's my new deal with the Universe. I will simply live.

Love J.

THE CAMINO LETTERS

I

Hi Julie:

AFTER MUCH THOUGHT, I DECIDED to copy you the words that were being read to Marty as we sat with him on July 2nd, 2004. About two lines from the end of this reading, he left this world peacefully.

The book is entitled *The Gift of Peace: Personal Reflections* by Joseph Cardinal Bernardin (Chicago: Loyola Press, 1997). It was given to us when Marty was ill and was read by all, including him, and became a source of strength and comfort for us.

Without further babbling, I quote:

What I would like to leave behind is a simple prayer that each of you may find what I have found — God's special gift to us all: the gift of peace. When we are at peace, we find the freedom to be most fully who we are, even in the worst of times. We let go of what is nonessential and embrace what is essential. We empty ourselves so that God may more fully work within us. And we become instruments in the hands of the Lord. As I have said so often, if we seek communion with the Lord, we must pray. One of my favorite prayers is

attributed to St. Francis of Assisi. Let us conclude by recit-
ing it together:

> Lord, make me an instrument of your peace.
> Where there is hatred, let me sow love.
> Where there is injury, pardon.
> Where there is doubt, faith.
> Where there is despair, hope.
> Where there is darkness, light.
> Where there is sadness, joy.
> O Divine Master, grant that I may not so much seek
> to be consoled, as to console;
> to be understood, as to understand;
> to be loved, as to love;
> for it is in giving that we receive,
> it is in pardoning that we are pardoned.
> It is in dying that we are born to eternal life.

I hope this is useful to you, as I know Marty tried in his own way
to live by this prayer.

I find it very calming and know it pretty well by heart.

Have a wonderful experience and please share with me on your
return.

God speed.

Mary Anne

RONCESVALLES, JULY 2, 2009

Dear Mary Anne:

AS I READ YOUR TASK at four o'clock this morning, on the first day of walking from St. Jean Pied de Port in France to Roncesvalles in Spain, I found it hard to believe that five years have passed since Marty's death. I was so lucky to move in his shadow in those years before he died, and I cannot say how much your task has touched me and sent me on my way.

Because Marty was so much larger than me (perhaps four times, would you say?), a joke began after a difficult day of argument in court when, back in the lawyers' lounge, I threatened to go jump off a bridge in protest, and Marty said he was coming with me. The joke was: "If Julie and Marty jumped off the Hunter Street Bridge at the same time, who would hit the water first?" The answer is that we would hit the water at the same time because of some amazing law of physics. How does that work?

There do not appear to be bridges here, at least not yet. Only mountains. The mountains that I walked through today are part of the Basque Country, which straddles France and Spain. The Basques have the oldest unwritten European language, Euskara, and the culture and politics in the region are fuelled by strong ties to a unique and ancient culture. The Basques are said to be the oldest European people, descended, perhaps, from the Cro-Magnons who produced the famous cave paintings in Spain and France. Basque women were considered to be witches in medieval times, and many of them probably were, with knowledge of the moon and the forest. The Basques, in general, stubbornly refused to convert to Christianity. Perpetually on the wrong side of history, the Basques were persecuted and prosecuted at the whim of the State. The Spanish Inquisition sought the Basque witches with a vengeance.

The most well-known Basque goddess is Mari, or "Lady Justice," who is said to appear as a shape shifter – sometimes an animal, sometimes a rainbow, sometimes a burning tree. How very like Lady Justice! Mari was the goddess of rain and drought, and she punished offenders with water. After the Spanish Inquisition, she was worshipped by the Basques side by side with the Virgin Mary: Mari / Mary. Who could tell the difference?

After the Renaissance, Lady Justice became the matron *Justitia*, who now stands throughout the world with her sword and scales and blindfold. I recall that Marty kept Lady Justice on his bookshelf. In mid-argument Marty would sometimes hold his massive arms out to each side, hands poking out of his flowing black gown – as though he were, himself, the scales of justice – urging the Court and all those in it to believe in innocence. He was a great defender, believing that the most wretched criminal should be visibly treated like a king by his own counsel as he walked into a courtroom to meet his presiding Justice.

Marty always told me to maintain the stance of the wide-eyed innocent. I have considered this statement often, and almost everything about it eludes me to this day. He also said that it is always best to use honey instead of vinegar: sweet as pie, so they don't see you coming. This is particularly true for me, because I am so small that they don't see me coming anyway. Marty always understood me.

When I was indeed a wide-eyed innocent, during my articles, a girl I had once known was before the criminal court after becoming ill with schizophrenia. She was living on the street, causing a ruckus, and had kicked a cop – not unusual among the crimes and misdemeanours that fill the criminal court. I was told that she came into court wearing her shoes on her hands, and walked in bare feet from the back of the courtroom to the bar where the accused is to stand before the court. There was laughter in the gallery, which was probably to be expected, and many of the lawyers waiting in the courtroom snickered and laughed along with the crowd.

I was so, so new to this world of law and had such a naïve belief in the core role of the advocate as a proponent of justice, that when I heard the story of the lawyers laughing at this poor woman who had once been so beautiful and sane, it sat heavy in the pit of my stomach and made me ache for her. I was so upset by it that I cried in Marty's office as I told him how disappointed I was that lawyers would laugh at her. "Burst" is a better word for what I did in his office – I sat opposite him with my head in my hands and sobbed.

I felt as I had felt the first time I heard someone screaming from downstairs in the prisoners' cells and watched the world in the courtrooms above carry on with the moving of paper and people's lives, as though the tortured screams were simply music in an elevator. I sat frozen, listening, and realized in a visceral way that the whole point of this exercise was to put human beings into cages and to try not to hear the screams.

Marty told me never to lose my emotion, and to make sure that I felt it and felt it deeply. There have most definitely been things I have seen in my practice of law that I have not been able to let pass without voluminous tears and anger. Never in court, though. Only in Marty's office. Or on a walk. Or in my car. Or behind my desk at night. And once, I recall, in Jim's office.

I have always been a Pollyanna, easily teased and quite soft. I used to grow vegetables at Trent Daycare when the girls were very small – long before law school. One of the lawyers in town had kids in the same daycare, and I think he felt sorry for me because I rode my bike with Malakai on the back. He also thought I was a "pinko" and told me so. Now a colleague, he told me not very long ago that he had been thinking about the garden and what a great thing it was. It was. We grew a huge pumpkin, and the kids were very excited about harvesting it for Hallowe'en. But just before Hallowe'en, on a Monday morning, we arrived at the day-care to find the pumpkin smashed in the street – no doubt tossed by some drunken students. Who would do that? What a cruel and horrible thing for toddlers to see. I cried buckets over that stupid pumpkin.

But that was a long time ago. I am much harder than that now, and it takes far more to make me cry. I have seen pictures of things beyond description. I know about the many ways in which people can and do commit suicide and what comes afterward. Young, middle-aged, elderly, sane and insane. It doesn't make much difference at that point.

I know what physical evidence of sexual assault looks like – in the young, the middle-aged, both male and female – and what technical issues apply to the evidence. I know of horrors witnessed by children who somehow are able to find the words to express it. And secrets held by the elderly and contained only in my files, as they quietly prepare for death.

I have seen what child pornography and murder look like, and I have heard endless details, emotions reduced to facts, facts reduced to evidence, lives reduced to issues of "relevance."

I have also seen professionals – persons whom society entrusts with the knowledge of these things – blatantly lie to cover up their own personal failures, inadequacies, addictions and, above all, their fear.

How do you maintain the stance of the wide-eyed innocent in the face of all that? I don't know how Marty did it. And I miss him because I can't ask.

Because of Marty, I have remembered to not think that I am simply being "like a girl" when I am upset about something that is indeed upsetting. In law, for a woman lawyer, it is quite common for things to be pushed aside on that basis.

As I walked today and thought about how disappointed and disillusioned I am with "Lady Justice," I missed Marty hugely with his great flowing arms and huge innocent heart, and I was grateful for him. Marty had a way of making everyone behave well, just by his presence. That was not clear to me until he died.

In the Pyrenees forest, I found myself mourning his death, which I now realize I had not done before. When he was sick, I cried many times in my car at the thought of him dying and how hard he worked to hide his suffering through all of the chemo treatments. I don't remember myself crying afterward, except in response to thinking of how much you and the girls and Sharon and Anne were missing him so. I do tend to cry about other people's sadness more than my own. My own sadness is much more efficient if I turn it into anger about something else. But here, five years later to the day, I cried (again burst, in fact) because I miss Marty terribly.

Did you know, when you gave me your task, that St. Francis of Assisi walked the Camino de Santiago in 1214? He did it twice, and I think he may have started in either St. Jean Pied de Port or Roncesvalles. I was in both places on your day. As we walked in the shadow of St. Francis, Malakai and I exchanged some harsh words at a crossing, and she tore ahead to join some younger and faster Brazilian pilgrims. I didn't know where exactly she had gone or if she had noticed the very faintly marked turn of the Camino through a sheep pasture, so for much of the day I was totally and completely consumed with fear and anxiety. I was alone, often in the woods, often on a difficult and narrow path, and there was nowhere to go but forward, with the thought of finding my child. Hardly a channel of peace.

You would not know that I am very familiar with the prayer you have given me, but I am. I have not thought of it for quite some time, but we sang it when I was a teenager at United Church youth retreats. Because of your task, "Make me a Channel of your Peace" began to play in my mind and continued on, with thoughts of Marty, for the rest of what was to be a difficult beginning day.

One of the things that I berated myself for as I walked through the endless forest was the fact that I am so terrible at sending thank-you notes. In fact, I don't know if I have ever sent one for any occasion, ever. I think that is a great sin. I always intend to, and I have boxes of lovely cream and gold thank-you cards that I bought after my brother died two years ago. But sitting and writing a card has not been something I have ever been able to force myself to do. If I am honest about this, I will tell you that I am frightened by grief and do not allow myself to go anywhere near it. But when my brother died I was so truly comforted by the cards from your family: you and the girls, Sharon and Fred, and Anne. And I have not said thank you. Thank you.

I was not expecting to be alone, and I was not expecting to be gripped by such fear. Yet, because I started my day with it, and because this was the task you gave me for this day, I sang myself up the Pyrenees and sang my way through my fear in the forest. Just words, but familiar ones from a long time ago, and with a rhythm that I could match to my footsteps.

As I sang my way up and down the hills, my mind again and again turned to Marty, and to Ted, the very gifted minister who organized the United Church youth retreats (and, for some bizarre reason, my mind was also filled with the word "propel"). These two men, now connected in my mind with this song, were extremely important to me at very different times. They would have liked each other, I thought. I considered the ways in which I have been propelled by each of them — by their example, by their words, and by their encouragement and love for me. It is an absolute fact that if Ted had not been so central to my teenage life, I would not have done any of what has come since. The same is true of Marty in the first years of my law life.

The church retreats back when I knew Ted were full of wonderful things, talk of peace and justice and love, and all the best people. I became involved by chance and it provided a much-needed refuge for me in the years between my mother's death and leaving home at seventeen. I remember one retreat where we were all placed in a large circle and Ted, along with others, washed our feet. Having Ted wash my feet was one of the most powerful experiences I have had, and I can still see Ted kneeling with the basin, looking up at me. The lesson was about humility and service. I was about fifteen, I think. Before asking him for a task for my Camino, I hadn't spoken to Ted in over twenty years.

What I was never sure of, back then, was the question of faith — or rather, the question of *my* faith. I was surrounded by the goodness of a progressive, socially conscious church and knew the gospel well. But I always felt like I was faking because I was never as sure as others seemed, like my friend Garth, who is the son of United Church ministers and missionaries, a math genius, and now a tenured professor. With Garth, it has always seemed to me that his faith in God with a capital "G" is as real and tangible to him as mathematics. Garth never got a math problem wrong. He said that if there is an answer to be found, as there is in math, it is easy — you just have to follow the steps. For Garth, I think God fit into the same category. I always, always, envied that.

I, on the other hand, was always wracked with questions

about the meaning of life and death and the universe, and why my mother had died, and why we have to die at all. Those questions have continued to this day. I'm sad to say that I have never progressed an inch in faith beyond the simple questions of a ten-year-old.

All that being said, I do have some churchy trappings behind me, so I understood and appreciated what you gave me to ponder over a distance of twenty-seven kilometres up and through the Pyrenees Mountains. I have not been physically training for this. I have not been mentally preparing for this. And I very quickly, on this day, came to appreciate the basic fact that I must begin, gain momentum, and keep going.

I never spoke with Marty directly about his spiritual life — all that I know of that, I know from you. But I have often thought of Marty going to the Church at Assumption just before he died simply to thank the congregation for their weekly prayers. And I think he went to explain the ways in which the prayers of this group of relative strangers had indeed landed in his life. I also often think of a particular day about two months before Marty died, when he and I were alone in the lawyers' lounge at Simcoe Street. In the middle of all of the business of the day, he told me that he had been asking himself what reason there could possibly be that we were born here while others are sitting on the sun-baked soil in Africa waiting for water. He was angry, and I rarely saw him angry. It has stayed with me because it is indeed a question that should be felt with such emotion. It is also a question of faith.

On the subject of jumping from the Hunter Street Bridge, I thought about the miraculous answer to the question for a fair amount of time while walking, trying to figure out how this law of physics could possibly be so. If the answer is that Julie and Marty would hit the water at the same time, then I think that just about anything is possible. This led to my thinking about the power of the universe. And whether there is a God. And whether Jesus was the Son of God. And then what about Buddha and Mohammed and Ganesha and the witches' moon? I suppose these are not bad questions to ask on the road from St. Jean Pied de Port to Roncesvalles – I think they have perhaps been asked here before!

The Prayer of St. Francis of Assisi is about allowing oneself to be emptied in order to then become a resonant vessel, filled by the Holy Spirit. Is this a question of faith or a question of physics? I don't understand physics. I tell my children that I have always been super-duper smart but that's not true – I think I almost failed grade-eleven physics. I'll have to ask Garth, the math genius of great faith. Garth has given me a task for the last day, so I'll have to hang on to all my math and science questions until I write to him.

The Pyrenees mountains were indeed beautiful, but it was all so, so difficult, with my thoughts and the long climb down into Roncesvalles at the end. On the climb upward, I was physically desperate to go back down. But when it was finally time to descend, it was so much more difficult than I expected. Again I sang to propel myself down into the small village. I sang the Prayer of St. Francis. I also sang "The Bear Went Over the Mountain" and "Ring Around the Rosy." If anyone was watching me, they would have definitely thought that something had become unhinged along the way. Crazy as it was – though I don't think Marty would have thought me crazy at all – singing was the only way I could keep going, and I was so grateful for having been given a song with your task, even though that is not what you had intended.

In Roncesvalles, entering on my rubber legs, I found my beautiful daughter lying in her sleeping bag, waiting for me under a tree.

I was both relieved and annoyed, as is often the case for a parent. I could not explain to her what I had gone through this day, after she abandoned me. My day of worry and fear was, to her, quite silly because obviously she was fine. I, on the other hand, was very slow, completely out of shape, and had to stop to pee in the bushes far too often. For this I was roundly chastised before supper by my very fast child who had been waiting under the tree for over three hours.

We settled into the Roncesvalles albergue, which sleeps over a hundred pilgrims in a cavernous room lined with bunk beds and strangers. This was a medieval pilgrims' hospital and has been used in this way since the twelfth century. The unwritten and unspoken rules were quickly developed regarding the hanging of laundry and the storage of packs. A girl from the Netherlands arranged for us to get two of the last tickets to the pilgrims' dinner, and we congregated for fish and wine. At 8:00 p.m., there was a pilgrims' mass in the church, where the priest gave an 800-year-old pilgrims' blessing. It was solemn and heartfelt, and after such a day, I knew that this was about being encouraged and sent forth – even though I am not Catholic, did not take Communion, and do not speak Spanish.

Individual preparations for the next day continued in the albergue. At the computer terminal, the girl from the Netherlands and I eventually discovered where the "@" symbol is on a Spanish keyboard. I checked my laundry and realized that it would not be dry by morning, as I had arrived too late. I had to pull out my safety pins so I can hang it all on my pack tomorrow to dry in the sun. Everyone else's clothes were dry, and I felt slightly defeated by my failure. Patience was required while waiting in the common area for an empty plug to charge the camera battery. While waiting, I was able to study the contents of two shelves of "stuff" that people had forgotten — all manner of things, mostly shampoo, books, some clothing. As I was scanning the shelves, I realized that these were not items forgotten; heavy and now deemed un-necessary, they had been discarded after the first hard day. I had not previously considered this. The idea that one could just "get rid of stuff" suddenly became hugely appealing.

I went back to the main area and into my bed where I began thinking of things I could leave behind too. I sorted and re-sorted in my mind, the way I think of my file lists as I'm going to sleep if I'm too overworked and too tired to cope otherwise. There have been many panicky days with too little done for too many files, running through the list, A–Z, on the verge of sleep. Each file, each problem, considered and checked, and then dreamt about. Sometimes I have stayed up all night working toward the quiet stillness of my 4:00 a.m. thoughts. Sometimes it has been worth it, but not always. Sometimes I have stayed up all night, tossing and turning, worrying for the safety of my client or myself. Or churning over ethical and moral dilemmas that I must solve alone.

I can't remember when exactly it was that I decided that going to sleep while running through file lists in my mind was no way to live, but it came to the point, last fall, when I quite abruptly got rid of all of my staff (effectively eliminating almost all of my overhead), and began working to slow it all down. I promised my-self that I would spend the month of July, while the kids were at camp, at home in my garden so I could catch my breath. That particular idea didn't quite work out — because it is now July, and I am here.

As I was continuing to ponder what I might leave behind, the lights went out and all good pilgrims went to sleep. That was my first day.

Love J.

2

Hi Julie:

YOUR MESSAGE SAYS YOU WILL be walking for twenty-six days and you want to have a task set or something to focus on for each of those days. Since you are working through the alphabet — I am day two. This is very early in your pilgrimage. I don't think you will have been challenged physically or mentally at this stage so....

You are a highly intelligent, motivated, energetic person. You set yourself goals and you have achieved them. You have your own law practice, a beautiful home, and your family is happy and well adjusted. I think on day two of your pilgrimage I should like you to try not to focus on the goal you have set — distance to travel that day for example or reaching Santiago de Compostela. But instead, try to let your mind be free to think about the millions who have travelled the very same path you are walking. And, the many reasons people undertake this physical challenge. Maybe you want to give thanks for all the good things in your life. Maybe you want to think about changes you may want to make. So on day two please try to be aware of your surroundings, enjoy the company of people you may encounter, and at the end of the day be happy no matter how far you have walked.

You will be in my thoughts.

Love to you and Malakai.

Love Barbara

p.s. I am not convinced that this will be the only time you will walk this path.

Dear Barbara:

AS I READ YOUR TASK this morning, I laughed out loud at the line "I don't think you will have been challenged physically or mentally at this stage," because day one was a doozy.

I walked twenty-seven kilometres, mostly uphill, with Malakai having charged ahead to God knows where – producing a day of physical exhaustion, loneliness, and fear. I thought at some point in the day about how much my parenting has been governed by fear, and I was sad for that. When Malakai was a very small baby and was sleeping in my bed, I stirred in the night and rolled over, not yet awake, just in time to catch her by her sleeper as she rolled and fell toward the floor. I didn't realize what had happened until I fully woke, holding her above the floor by the back of her sleeper. When she was about one and a half years old, she choked on a candy and turned blue. By instinct and fear, I flipped her upside down and pounded her back enough to pop the candy out. I still, to this day, would prefer that she not eat hard candies. When she was about two, she ate poison berries and we had to go to the hospital where she had to drink eight ounces of pure charcoal. I, as her mother, had to pour it down her throat. We were both covered in black and she was as angry as a two year old can be.

A helpful nurse produced an orange popsicle. Orange popsicles are always a good thing, but sometimes they are not enough.

I wasn't worried when Malakai first left me on the Camino. She had been annoyed with me for being slow, and I was annoyed with her for being so critical of me as I struggled so hard to keep up. I told her that it was not my fault, actually, that I had to stop to pee in the bushes every half hour. My bladder is not used to this and I am forty. She thinks I am ridiculous, but perhaps one day she'll understand.

When she raced ahead I was relieved at first to be able to walk at my own pace. The Camino is clearly marked with yellow arrows and scallop shells, so I thought it was impossible to get lost. Then I came to a place where the path along the road veered to the right and moved uphill through a sheep pasture, barely visible. The turn was marked by a small yellow arrow on a rock, which I missed. I noticed other pilgrims behind me turning off, so I turned back and found my way behind them.

This, of course, made me afraid that Malakai had carried on down the wrong road. I spent the day going forward with the mission to find her. I sang the prayer of St. Francis of Assisi, part of my task for the first day and oddly familiar from my youth-group days, and I sang my way along and forward. I also sang "The Bear Went Over the Mountain" several times. These things — my lost child and St. Francis of Assisi — were the only reason I was able to walk so far on the first day, having arrived in St. Jean Pied de Port completely and totally unprepared for this.

I AWOKE THIS MORNING IN THE Roncesvalles albergue to the sound of monks chanting a Gregorian chant. We were lined up on bunks in a huge room in what used to be a medieval pilgrims' hospital in the twelfth century. It felt, as I woke, that the monks were there beside me, singing. It was a recording, but it filled the room beautifully and completely.

The Roncesvalles albergue is, I think, the only one like it on the Camino, and it marks the beginning. There was a pilgrims' mass in Spanish, with an 800-year-old pilgrims' blessing that is said every night for each fresh crop of pilgrims, as it has been for hundreds of years. How fitting that this should be on the eve of your day.

The pilgrims' blessing was read in English by a priest with such a thick Spanish accent that the only word I was able to hear was, I think, "symphony." I don't know if that was it, but that is what I heard, and I found it interesting because one of my recurring thoughts is simply three words: "solo," "harmony," "symphony." I must request a copy of the text of the blessing if I can find out whom to ask. I did find a book that described the pilgrims' blessing as being open to all, sick and well, Catholic and pagan, Jews, heretics, and vagabonds. But I still want to find the real text.

In the albergue, the volunteer *hospitalieros* assigned us bunk beds and took our shoes. I didn't take a picture of the shoes all lined up on shelves against the wall, which is something that I now regret. I often think I should take more pictures. But, at the same time, I remember being at a workshop once with a medical doctor, obviously a super-achiever, who took pictures constantly and obsessively. He described to me in great detail the sadness he always felt when looking at the pictures later, because he never was able to capture the moment the way he wanted to. The problem with this was obvious to me, but not at all to him. It made me wonder what things are obvious to others, and not to me. The mind is a very funny trap.

The night before your day, I slept soundly, being forced like a child to go to bed at ten, when all of the lights were turned out and the unspoken rules of the Camino would forbid anything but sleep. I have not slept so well in a very long time. It was a good tired, as they say — the product of many, many hours of hard slogging.

And so, on July 3, I awoke in the most beautiful way. The Gregorian chant echoed through the huge space. Quietly, people around me stirred, whispering to their companions if they were not travelling alone, in a dozen languages, whispering and packing. The many, many people who are indeed travelling alone were silent. All I could hear around me was the music and the rustling of packs and shoes as we all prepared to head out into the mist.

I put my pack on, and it felt heavier than the first day. My thighs and my groin and my shoulders hurt. My upper shoulder was chafed from the pack, which now rested in the same painful place. I was in pain, but there was nothing to do but get going. I couldn't lounge in bed all day in the albergue because they kick you out at 8:00 a.m. Where was I to go but forward? As we left the albergue, we were met by the volunteer *hospitalieros* who had cared for us. They said *"Buen Camino,"* and off we went.

The phrase *Buen Camino* is now familiar — it is the standard greeting among all pilgrims as you pass, or let pass, on the path. But it was a surprise to me on the first day as I have never been wished a good journey before, in that way, with such sincerity.

The path on your day was from Roncesvalles to Zubiri. The first village on the way was Burgette, where Hemingway used to fish, and where there was café con leche after about a one-hour walk. Malakai slowed for me for most of the day, and when she went ahead she left her blue bandana on one of the pilgrims' rock piles so that I knew she had gone in the right direction — a sharp turn to the right.

I did not turn my mind to Santiago de Compostela once. This was not only because of your task; perhaps it had even more to do with the lingering exhaustion. The only goal I wanted to achieve today was to convince Malakai to carry the toilet paper George talked me into bringing in my pack. We also had a small discussion regarding who would carry the baguette we purchased in Burgette. The solution was to eat the baguette completely and leave the toilet paper at the next stop. A few sheets taken in the morning were all that was needed.

I did indeed let my mind wander. Although the path itself was not as physically demanding as the path through the Pyrenees, my muscles ached and I began the day wondering what I had done. I chastised myself for not being more prepared, for packing too much to carry, for leaving behind so many responsibilities, for setting out on this frivolous, painful walk. To what end? For what?

I often think of the phrase "For what?" because of a favourite client of mine. When he first came to the office it was after the death of his wife of almost sixty years. They had been postwar refugees who moved to Canada, worked hard at two jobs or more, lived frugally, and saved a small fortune. He sobbed in my office as he talked about his wife, whom he had loved dearly. His greatest regret was that they had never taken a trip anywhere. About the money he now had in the bank, he said: "For what?!" I will never forget his agony, and his phrase is something I often quietly ask clients when they are at cross purposes with the decisions they must make to move forward: "For what?" Of course, I have rarely asked this of myself.

As I walked past Burgette, the pain in my groin was unbearable, and I felt very sorry for myself for being so weak and sore. After a while, I turned my mind to your task, which was to stop thinking about myself and to think of the millions of people who have walked this same route, for their own reasons, before me. That helped.

In the Basque Country, where I am, there were witches and vampires and cannibals (oh, my). And the Inquisitors who pursued them. Napoleon and Charlemagne both came over the same mountain path I did yesterday, in their time and in war. And then there was the odd-duck hermit who had a vision and followed the twinkling stars and music down this path in the ninth century to find the decapitated bones of St. James, at what was to become Santiago.

The story is that St. James was martyred in Jerusalem and beheaded. His body and the bodies of two of his disciples were put in a stone boat that sailed unattended for seven days until it arrived at the River Ulla on the Spanish coast at Compostela. Thus the hermit made the Way of St. James, and here we are. And yet, long before that – perhaps a millennium before – the Celts followed the same route, under the Milky Way, in search of the Sun god at the end of world: Finisterre. Santiago has the cathedral; Finisterre has the rocks on which fertility rites were performed before the Sun god. Perhaps it is all part of the same thing?

It is not an obviously religious pilgrimage for most of the people I have met so far, which has made me consider the whole idea of "pilgrimage." What is it, if not religious? Some pilgrims talk only in the number of kilometres travelled per day – a marathon day after day and a badge to carry. Most, it would appear, are simply walking, simply drawn, perhaps searching and indeed propelled toward something. Toward what? Indeed, *for* what? Somewhere, between here and Santiago, maybe each pilgrim will find a reason. But it's not about Santiago. Santiago is not a destination, at least not in my mind. It is the place at the end of what is the in-between. That is how I am feeling today, on day two.

Pilgrimage is a universal ritual experience. The third ashrama in the Hindu circle of life is Vanaprastha, a gradual detachment from the material world through pilgrimage. It promises the truth that late in life all people are finally travelers — wanderers free from taxes, free from property, free from raising children, concerned with other, spiritual things. What an interesting thought for me, who is so mired in law, so buried in paper and problems and rules and responsibilities. I am not free. I am not a pilgrim. I am still raising children. George and I have managed to raise these four beautiful children, and we are not yet done. However, it does appear that for this short time, I have nothing to do but walk.

By mid-day, I felt as though I was utterly surrounded by butterflies. There were so many, and I stopped on a steep hill to watch them. I tried to photograph them as they danced. When I looked at the photographs that I took, the butterflies in the pictures were simply white light. They were moving too fast, or were simply too luminous, to be captured by the camera. I had to dance with them to try to take a picture, and there was definitely a goal in this: I was trying to get a picture of the butterflies dancing so that I could show you the magic of it, but I succeeded only in capturing their light.

Later in the afternoon, I was speaking at some length with a young German girl who was travelling alone and obviously struggling with her very large and heavy pack. I was telling her about dancing with the butterflies on the steep climb, and she talked about how much she loved butterflies and that her childhood nickname had been caterpillar.

We then talked about childhood, and I told her about the Dandelion Club that my neighbour, Agnes, belonged to. Agnes was my tormentor and remained so forever. To get into the Dandelion Club you had, of course, to spell the word "dandelion."

I won all of the spelling bees in grade two; I was a smarty-pants and could even spell "photosynthesis." But I misspelled "dandelion" in my desperate endeavour to get into the club, even though the clubhouse was only made of sticks and garbage bags. It was a tragedy.

Later, when I was going to sleep, I thought of the last butterfly I chased through Ravi Naimpally's raspberry canes when I was six, and I saw myself and Ravi racing around the backyards, which were not divided by a fence. Since I was never part of the Dandelion Club, that was the sort of thing that I did. It was a huge butterfly – black and white – and Ravi and I caught it in a two-litre Mason jar. I don't know what happened to it after that. I hope it escaped.

Ravi's father was a math professor at the University. They were from Mumbai and were very exotic for Thunder Bay in the 1970s. They had a small shrine in their basement behind a velvet curtain – I think the curtain was red, and whatever was behind it had a very particular smell. I only peeked a couple of times because it scared me.

I told the young German girl that two friends had recently called me "grasshopper," which I found odd and funny. It was my lawyer friend Sue who started it. I asked her to comment on the bio materials for my still-to-be-up-and-running new website. She told me that I needed one line to sum it all up. I replied by email that this was the hard part. Her response back to me was, "The answer is in what you have already written, grasshopper." George thinks this is all a retro-reference to *Kung Fu*, but I am too young to remember that.

The German girl and I passed the time, and the up and down of the trail, talking about insects and butterflies. What a pleasure it was, despite the difficulty I had in trying to explain the word "propel," which did not appear to have a direct translation in German. We were, of course, speaking of the difficult day before and the need to lighten one's load. I suggested that this was a metaphor for life itself, and she said something very wise: "Before you know the need, you need to have the experience." So true.

And so the road to Pamplona is one of tired and sore pilgrims, spending their footsteps with thoughts of what they no longer wish to carry. Need takes on a very different meaning when you physically carry it on your back. There are moments when all I want and need is my water sac. The rest is too much, and I could easily leave it all behind.

As I walked alone, later in the day, I did indeed turn my mind to all of the goals I have had and achieved, as you said. You have been there for much of that during some very formative and busy years. I have been so lucky to have you. I don't know what I would have done without you when we found out that we were going to lose Alexander. I thought of him today, opened it up just a crack. I wrote yesterday to Marty's wife, in response to her task for the first day, that I am frightened of grief. And I am.

So all of the goals and all of the successes and failures, balance and lack of balance, plans and lists and crises, have kept me very, very busy. I am proud of all of it, true. Give me something to do and I'll do it. Tell me what you need and I'll give it. Tell me I can't do something and I'll show you. But I am very tired, and my body is screaming for me to stop and rest. And that is what I'm doing here, though it doesn't feel like rest to me today. It hurts.

I kept thinking of something said to me quite recently: "Just because you can, doesn't mean you have to." Instead of goals to achieve, I tried today to open my mind to choices that can be made with each step, each thought. Just because you can, doesn't mean you have to. Just because you can carry it on your back, doesn't mean you have to. This is the road to Pamplona, and it is all about choosing what to carry on the longer road to Santiago.

On this day, I thought of you (of course). I thought of your strong running legs, and your goodness and playfulness and laughter. Through my own weary legs, walking and thinking, I was grateful for you. I can still see you as you were the first time I met you at the University all those years ago – walking across the quad toward me. I told George that night after I had met you that I couldn't figure out whether you were six or fifty-six. Before I left to come here, Malakai and I were driving in Peterborough and we saw you striding down Charlotte Street. We said: "Look, there's Barbara." We knew you from a distance, because of your walk. And today I have decided that it is most definitely because of the way you move through this world – like a beautiful dancing butterfly.

Love J.

3

Hi Julie

MY TASK FOR YOU IS a "mind pallette" cleanser of sorts,
perhaps best done when at rest at a quiet time. It will cleanse your
mind to prepare for the next task and open your mind to new
visual experiences.

Close your eyes and imagine to be inside a closed space
with no corners or edges such as in an egg or ball. You are
floating in this soft space.

Now also think of only one colour that gives a soft glow to
the inside of this space, you are totally surrounded by this
one colour, floating inside the soft space.

Now also think of one note/tone, mentally hum this one
note. You are surrounded by this one note and the one
colour, floating inside the soft/rounded space.

Do this at least once a day for at least ten minutes. If you wish you may change the colour and the note each day, but not the space.

Have a great time!

Agda

Dear Agda:

OF COURSE IT IS NO surprise that you were one of the very few taskmasters who did not stay within the confines of a single day, but rather gave me a task for each day of the whole journey. You are also one of only three people I have ever known who has reached with an open hand toward me and squeezed my face. A very bold gesture.

Therefore I did start your task on the very first day, even before I started walking. I have my egg. I have my sky-blue sky. Those two things have not changed. And I have my flute.

On June 30, after landing in Paris, I took the train and listened to my "Don't Stop Me Now" Queen playlist, which was completely ridiculous. I was full of anxiety, worried that I would miss the connection to Bayonne. I don't speak French. It is such a crime that I don't speak French when my mother was Franco-Ontarian and didn't speak English until age fifteen. I wish I could ask her why. But she's long dead.

The train-ticket lady told me to validate *le billet* in the little yellow thing on the track. I didn't. I was afraid of the machine and couldn't read the instructions. I was worried about other things, like missing the train and finding my seat in French. Then I became worried about my invalidated *billet*. I am a worrier.

I was also tired. The plane ride was long and uncomfortable. I was sandwiched between two beautiful women — one an Iranian

PhD student off to hike in the Pyrenees. In my journal that day I noted, "Pyrenees – where is that?" I am therefore certifiably a complete idiot, because my first day of walking was through the Pyrenees and I had no clue where I was even going before I started to walk. My excuse is that I decided only three weeks before I got on the plane that I was going to do this.

The other woman sitting beside me was a middle-aged Chinese woman who asked if she could have my airplane muffin for her husband. I imagined the woman and her husband having a small and celebratory muffin picnic somewhere, at her final destination, which was not Paris.

I spent too much on a taxi to the train station. George had told me to take the metro, and when I said I was nervous about getting from the airport to the train on time without taking a taxi, he called me "chicken shit." I don't think that is a very nice thing for a husband to say. Especially a husband who told me on the same day, "Remember that I love you for being the pure spirit of light that you are!" Those two things appear to be contradictory, don't you think? Why is marriage like that?

Anyway, I was glad to take a taxi because the packs were heavy – I was carrying both Malakai's and mine. It did dawn on me, while making this decision based on the heaviness of the packs, that I would be carrying one of them on my back for a month. As I write this, I have now carried my pack for three days and I hate it. It hurts me. I can't lift my neck. One of my tasks much later on, from my friend Sylvia, is to look two feet above my head all day. I tried today to see if I could do it and I can't. I can't say that I'm looking forward to that failure.

Nothing is air conditioned here, and people happily sweat. In Paris, I watched a group of friends meet at the Gare de Mont-parnasse to travel together somewhere. One by one they arrived, and as each person came to the group the men shook hands and the women were kissed. No one was missed and there was no apparent discomfort in the touching. The only person I have in my life who does this to me consistently is Joe. And you, of course, squeezing my face. But there is very little physical contact in Canadian life. I watched these people greet each other with such ease and warmth, and I thought about Canada the cold. What would these people think watching the masses at Union Station? They would find it disquieting, perhaps — a scene from *Invasion of the Body Snatchers.* I have had those moments in Union Station while pausing to rustle in my bag for my phone or a piece of gum. I have looked up, frozen and facing the wrong direction, watching and feeling the swarms move past me, joylessly moving from office to train. I wish there was more dancing in the world. I should dance more. Now that I have no staff, I do sometimes dance in my empty office as I work.

Watching these people in Paris, I had a small ache for my now elderly aunts, Franco-Ontarian sisters of my mother, who are gathering themselves this weekend and who are more warm and sweaty and messy in life and relationships than the Anglo world. But that's as far as it goes. Very few people would ever greet me with a kiss. Except for my husband, no one could ever possibly be that happy to see me. And then there is the potential for germs and swine flu that would come with all that kissing and proximity. Pure Canadian ice — it's an interesting thing.

In the train station in Paris, there were birds jumping from table to table in the little café — tiny little wren creatures, eating crumbs and moving on. It made me think of the hawk that rests in my freezer. Why I would tell you this, I don't know. But I do have a hawk that has been in my freezer since March — a gift from my husband, who is probably the last person you would expect to offer such a thing. I have no doubt that I will find out what I am to do with it before the end of the summer, and then I will explain. It's a long story.

Women in France are beautiful and walk with straight and sure backs. I notice this each time I am here. And the older women are beautiful too – they are wrinkled and they smile with crooked teeth and without the obvious strain of Botox. Slight imperfections, at least among the middle-aged, appear to be tolerated without orthodontics. But maybe I just feel like I fit in here because of the Franco-nose and the crooked teeth. I did not have braces at fourteen, though I begged for them. My dad did not pay for things like that. I don't think he ever had a clue what my university tuition cost was or how many student loans I had. But he did buy me a car that was previously owned by my brother and gave me emergency money when we bought our house, so indeed he helped to cover what he knew to be the basic essentials as my life grew.

I did not miss the connection from Bordeaux to Bayonne. I sat on the train quite satisfied that I had managed to manoeuvre myself into the right place with my invalid *billet* and would see Malakai soon. She is such a brave child to have launched herself into the world, surrounded by language not hers, at seventeen. I am still far too shy and skittish about such things. I sat next to a little French girl on the train and did not take the opportunity to speak to her in French. I could have said something like "je ne parle pas français parce que ma mère parle français jusqu'à elle a quatorze ans et then never again" (how do you say that?). Never again. And then never again. I'll have to ask Malakai.

I could have said, "Quand j'avais dix-sept ans, j'avais un ami. Il s'appelait Gyslain. Il parle français, mais je travaille pour il étude anglais, not me – I was too shy. Et maintenant, Gyslain étude espagnol pour il va à Ecuador avec les étudiantes." Most of that, of course, makes no sense because I do not know the language. Gyslain does. He and I should have walked long enough, all of those days that we walked while on Canada World Youth, for me to learn French too. We only spoke English, and he ended up bilingual.

To the girl on the train, I said nothing at all in French. And then she pulled out a very sweet "My Trip to Great Britain" book and started to practise the English exercises. I still didn't speak. That is completely ridiculous. I must be more brave.

I read my twenty-six tasks through so I could start yours in my little blue egg rocketing through Europe. A friend gave me a beautiful piece of art that hangs in the front of my office. It reads:

> To live content with small means; to seek elegance rather than luxury; and refinement rather than fashion; to be worthy, not respectable; and wealthy, not rich; to work hard, think quietly, stride forward, talk gently, act frankly; to listen, to forgive, to act, flourish, guide, with open heart; to bear all cheerfully, to do all bravely, await occasion, hurry never; let the unbidden and unconscious grow up through the common. To this I aspire. This is my symphony.

There is an egg under the word *refinement*, and I have chosen this as my space. This egg.

The woman ahead of me in the train was crying. It made me upset for her. I wanted to reach ahead and rub her shoulder but I didn't. I think it's the pain that sticks to us, or it is what gets in the way. Other animals don't carry so much. They are slick. They have fur.

As the plane touched down in Paris, my first thought upon waking was "I quit." Quit what? I have never quit anything in my life, ever. Tell me I can't do it, and I'll show you. A former friend once said to me, "Everyone is waiting for you to hit a brick wall because it's impossible for someone to have as much energy as you do." Oh yeah? There is no brick wall. There is no limit. I'll show you!

But still I ask of my dreamtime: "Quit what?" And the answer that comes, from where I don't know, is this: *Enough of all that. Say it out loud.*

Yet even as I write this letter to you, the vampires creep in and threaten me with silence:

Who do you think you are? Agda doesn't care about what you think of her task! You asked for it, she gave it to you. So just do it already, and shut up. Don't go blah blah blahing about it. One of your friends even gave you the task of not talking about yourself for one whole day. Ha! Try that!!

What are you doing? You have a full life, a full law practice, a stack of bills you didn't bother to pay before you left and real tasks to do — did you even look at your real to-do list before you left? And you decide on a whim three weeks ago to leave? Who is going to take care of all that? Why are you doing this anyway? For what? And you think it's a good idea to do this with your seventeen-year-old daughter who only recently suggested that you needed to learn some parenting skills. Are you crazy?

How can I answer the vampires, Agda? *Who do you think you are?* I can't remember. That's why I'm here. I'm not an idiot. I have not lost my mind. I am someone who is brave enough to do this. Thank God, I am here.

Three years ago, at age thirty-seven, I hit the vampires' brick wall with my eyes. My body turned on itself, no longer able to distinguish between "self" and "non-self." My inflamed iris straining from within, white blood cells popping and shedding from the pressure. Autoimmune inflammation of the iris is now constant, and my right eye has been almost lost twice. I dare you, universe, to make me blind. I'll show you! My friend Christine, a magical drummer, calls this the "pain portal."

I have talked to you about this, or at least some of this, over strawberries and cream at Joe's just after the second time I came close to losing my eye. I don't really talk about it very deeply, very often — and I appreciated our conversation very much. It was after that, I think, that you started squeezing my face.

It's funny how we talk about disease (dis-ease, not easy), rather than death. Mortality is ever erased, rubbed away with fear. Life becomes deathless. Until you must face it.

In my family, life is deathful and the inability of the body to accurately perceive the self is a common problem. It's not a pre-determined death sentence necessarily, but a definite probability for some heavy-duty issues. I can't remember which specialist took my family history and said, "Well, it sure sucks about the bad genes." Dead mother. Dead brother. Eldest sister with chronic pancreatitis and plantar fasciitis, likely autoimmune. Next eldest sister with chronic sarcoidosis of the heart, definitely autoimmune. Two more sisters who are following my dad's risk factors, not mine. And my dad, who is as good as he can be at eighty-two with the plugged-up veins that he has.

Finally there is me, the baby girl — with the bad genes and eyes that are very prone to popping like popcorn. I exist knowing at my core that my life as it has been makes me an autoimmune freight train.

There is a word on the Camino, *Ultreia*, which means "Onward, Ho!" – and that's about what it comes down to. What can I do? Onward, ho.

My problem is that I have struggled to move onward from a particular point in my life and career in a radically different way, and it is not easy. This is a time in life, my mid-life, where there are so many responsibilities and so much inertia pushing me from behind. Janette said to me at the Kennedy's party in June, "Sometimes you don't know what to keep and what you need to let go of." That's for sure.

Harald inserted himself into my task list, which he had heard about from Grace. He didn't give me a task, but he did give me Oliver Schroer's *Hymns and Hers* to take with me. I was listening to the "Hymn for the Dispossessed" the night before I left. It is beautiful music. I listened to it again today, with your task in mind, and tried to hear each note. Then I listened to *Camino*, which was Schroer's recording made on the pilgrimage. It was so different to listen to it after three days of walking. It made me feel quite insignificant and large at the same time.

I also have with me, on my iPhone, a recording of Tibetan singing bowls that I borrowed from the naturopath who has converted me to acupuncture. I am very sensitive to acupuncture. I can feel, and she can see, the needles vibrate when they are sticking in me, or out of me, however it works. She has ordered very fine needles from Japan for me and they go deeper and further into whatever it is that they touch. I can feel it when they have gone deep enough and then I feel them start to move. The singing bowls play in the background most of the time that this happens. I have come to love the singing bowls and I have brought them with me. I listened to them today.

My brother had an arteriovenous fistula in his forearm when he was having dialysis and you could hear and feel the blood rush in it where the artery had been brought up to the surface of the skin behind his elbow. I love acupuncture because I know, from hearing my brother's fistula, that the acupuncture needles are somehow touching that sound and quiver. Isn't that an odd thought?

It leaves me with the feeling that none of it is about me, except my feet and what they do. And it's not about feeling sorry for others either. Pity is a useless emotion — completely self-gratifying and sanctimonious. Pity is the other side of contempt.

I DID FIND MALAKAI IN BAYONNE, despite the invalid *billet*, and we made our way to St. Jean Pied de Port. I was happy to be with her for two reasons: (a) she is fun, and (b) she thinks I am ridiculous and so does not want to be with me the whole time. She cannot believe that I am carrying a cedar flute, particularly now when so much of our time is spent planning what we will ship home at the first opportunity. But I will continue to carry my flute, and I am going to try to learn a new note each day. I have the instructions on my iPhone.

When I was young and learning to play piano with my mother, I had some talent and would always race ahead. As a result, my technique suffered and bad habits are hard to break. You have given me the task of focusing on one note each day, and I have chosen to do this through the music of Oliver Schroer and through my own flute. The result is that I am learning to play the flute slowly, purposefully, and carefully.

I have had this flute since March when Mary, Kiki, and I went on a cruise. The "woo woo cruise" or "woo woo afloat" as we call it, because there was a spiritual seminar on the cruise that I had registered for. I did this because I knew one of the presenters. I met her in October and she sent me a Christmas card. George took the Christmas card and found the website for the cruise and told me to go. He told me to go on the Camino too, through an email that had only a link to a website, followed by another email that said, "Go... now...."

He tells me to do a lot of things, it seems. And yet I regularly think that my husband does not understand me. Who am I kidding?

And so, doing what I was told, I went on the woo-woo cruise and ended up in a drum-circle exchange in Portobello, Panama, with conga dancers and drummers in a very small community hall. It was organized by Christine, who travels the world with her drum. It was awkward at times, in such a small space, with so much in it. One of our interpreters was Patricia Elena, a Panamanian jazz singer and pianist. She is beautiful and has a beautiful voice. As the energy in the room was building with the drums, an American woman stood and began to play her flute, this flute that I am carrying. She had not planned to play, but she did. And Patricia Elena began to sing. Patricia Elena is blind and so she could not see the spectacle. She could only feel. The drummers fell in behind her song, and the music began to weave between the flute and Patricia Elena's voice. It is difficult to explain the sound in that room, but there was a moment when the flute hit a high note and her voice met it perfectly, and it was exquisite. That is the only word I can think of to describe it — exquisite. This one note produced tears, and afterward one of the ten-year-old conga dancers described the feeling to Christine as this: "God is here."

That experience and your task have led me to many rangy thoughts. I remember reading about the Rosslyn Chapel in England, which was built by the Knights Templar, and the fact that patterns carved in the chapel have been proven to be related to musical notes, to be read in a specific order. This has led to a piece of music called "The Rosslyn Motet," played in the chapel not long ago with medieval-style instruments.

It was Chladni, in the seventeenth century, who first discovered, by covering a metal plate with sand and drawing a violin bow vertically across it, that sound vibrations produced physical geometric forms. The plate was bowed until it reached resonance and the sand then formed a pattern. A millennium ago, certain African tribes used the taut skin of the drum sprinkled with sand to divine the future. Egyptians thought of geometry as being "frozen music." There is a mathematical formula or explanation for this having to do with the crest and trough of sound waves, but I don't understand math. The higher the frequency, the more complex the shapes formed. There is a physics theory that even a single molecule of air or water carries all of the information required to describe the qualities and intensity of a given sound. I have a friend who is a math genius so I'll have to remember to ask him about this.

An English chemist did a similar thing with light, which produced crispations on tracing paper. One of my favourite quotations is from a Welsh woman who played with a wooden resonating chamber in the eighteenth century and created what she called "voice figures." She said, "I have gone on singing into shape these peculiar forms, and stepping out of doors, have seen their parallels in the flowers, ferns and trees around me...."

Someone is now working to capture vibrations in the water, so that they can catch the songs of whales and dolphins. Frozen music in the water. Imagine that. What if our very bodies were frozen music? Could we sing then? I so wish that I could sing.

I can't sing, but I do have my flute. It is large and thus the object of Malakai's exasperation. I have refused to carry the shampoo because I must carry the flute. Your day was the last stretch to Pamplona, with the hope of divesting ourselves of most of our belongings that quickly became too heavy to carry. And so my refusal to carry shampoo was understandably incomprehensible in light of the large cedar flute strapped to the bottom of my pack. I've wrapped the flute in Kiki's field hockey socks for protection; Kiki's at camp in Ontario and doesn't know this. I hope that she doesn't mind. I love her so, for her quiet, immense strength.

On the woo-woo cruise, there was a couple who played music to water and then sold the water, which they believe holds the vibration of love. I was given little stickers, which are intended to be stuck on the vessels that you drink this water from. Of course, this became a small joke with my children because who could believe that water could hold love's vibration? And yet, one evening I came back to our cabin and in the bathroom found one of the little stickers on a glass shelf beside my moisturizing cream: "gratitude." I love my children with all of my heart — all of them, with all of my heart. I can hold love, and I am ninety per cent water.

The reason I have the flute is another bit of magic from that trip. At the end of it all, Christine decided to raffle her drum to raise money for a hoped-for return to Iraq, where she had been with her drums in 2005. She talked about an Iraqi woman who said to her that she did not know how to pour out her pain until she started drumming. I don't feel that way about drumming at all, but maybe it's just that I'm too awkward and haven't done it enough. My friend Sylvia is taking drum lessons and has taken to it like a fish to water.

On the cruise, the drum was raffled off and then spontaneously Christine began drawing raffle tickets for "woo woo stuff," like reflexology balls and things that people were pulling out of nowhere and throwing into the ring. I can't remember what I got. I think it was a fortune-telling mirror or something. But when the

American woman stood up to auction her flute, I had a true mission. The auction ended, the flute was mine — and another man in the room matched the total raised in those forty-five amazing minutes. Christine and her video team spent April in Iraq, and I came home with my flute.

Before Christine left for Iraq, she mentioned something to me about a peacock feather. I knew where to get a peacock feather, of course, and called Evelyn. Evelyn gave me the feather and told me about being in Portobello two years ago during a huge conga festival — undoubtedly with the same children dancing the same 400-year-old slave-freedom dances. And thus the world continues to spin. I sent the feather to Christine and she brought me back a white feather and Sufi prayer beads, which I have with me here in my pack. I have not yet found out what happened to the peacock feather, but I'll have to ask. They say that a peacock must eat a thousand thorns to grow its plume. I wonder if that's true.

The Sufi prayer beads rest in my pack beside a rosary that belonged to my friend Felice's mother. These are just things, just stuff — but for some reason these are things I want to carry. I can do without the shampoo. The shampoo is not connected to anything.

I have tried very hard each day to find a quiet spot alone, to play my flute. In St. Jean Pied de Port I left Malakai at the albergue and I was brave enough to take my flute to the top of the Citadel. There I found a beautiful tree with a perfect root seat. I practiced playing up and down the flute, squeakily. I did the lesson from the iPhone and, as with everything, my tendency is to race onto the next, having been "good enough" at the first. But I listened to one note. I closed all of the holes on the flute and I played one note, thinking that perhaps sometimes one note is enough. One taste, one smell, one note....

The pace is so very different here, and I feel all of my clients and all of the needs of my home world falling off me. The human tragedies are sticky, but I do not need to carry them here. I am enjoying having so much time alone.

After the Citadel, I took myself to a small restaurant called "Cote Tart." The streets were empty because pilgrims must be in bed at ten or be locked out in the street. It was very quiet, with a fountain somewhere, jazz in the background, and the church bell ringing nine. When the bells rang the lights went out and the owner had to play with the fuse box.

ON THE WAY TO PAMPLONA today, I thought that I had no real work to do. I didn't have to get up and read your task, as I have been doing with the others, because your task carries through from day to day. But as it turned out, the day was absolutely filled with music and I returned again and again to the task of trying to listen to one note at a time, wherever there was music.

We arrived in a small town for lunch and came upon a wedding party in the street, singing. Later, on the path, I heard music in the distance and as I approached I saw two men standing outside a parked car, playing for the pilgrims from an overpass as we walked below. It was late in the day and I was tired and sore. I stopped to sit and listen and it made me weep for the simple kindness of it.

Here, in Pamplona, the post office is closed and we cannot ship our things. We now have to keep carrying the same weight to Logrono, so we have thrown out everything that can be disposed of in good conscience: the cardboard wrapper for the extra shoelaces, the facial wipes, and all the unnecessary pieces of paper. I threw out the extra photocopy of Malakai's passport, for example, because I thought it to be too heavy. Imagine thinking that paper is too heavy! My world is filled with paper. I am buried in paper. I have never thought of it as heavy before, but I suppose it is. Music is much, much lighter than the paper, even if my flute is big.

Coming back from the locked post office, I was unhappy. But, while walking through the square, I heard nothing but music and my bad mood could not last. Pamplona is getting ready for the running of the bulls, which starts tomorrow. We came upon an impromptu choir outside of a bar, singing harmony. It was truly spontaneous and beautiful. We also saw some boys who were playing a wooden xylophone with blocks of wood. The music has continued all night, through the open window of the hostel. A symphony ... so much music....

Earlier in the day, thinking about music and sound and vibration, the thought of "one note" began to intrigue me – the extension of this being a notion of universality of thought, or feeling, or desire. It is an odd thing to be on a path that has been travelled by millions of others, over centuries, in one direction. Why? And why am I doing this when my bones ache and I have work to do at home, managing all that heavy paper? And why do I think that these random thoughts, these tasks, these steps of mine, have any meaning or purpose to them at all?

It is singular. Solitary. One note. Mine.

In pondering these things while I walked, I kept returning to the universality of music, the ringing of a bell (which is a constant here), the marking of time, and returning to a single note, a single step, and beginning there. I am here.

Love J.

4

Hey Julie,
I AM REALLY EXCITED YOU ARE doing this.
It is a dream of mine.
Some suggestions:

a) when I run I often sing the spiritual:

> *Guide my feet, Love*
> *while I run this race*
> *Guide my feet, Love*
> *while I run this race*
> *'Cause I don't want to run this race in vain.*

b) one of my mantra prayers is:

> *Creator, create in me*
> *Spirit, inspire me*
> *Incarnation, be embodied in me*

c) one of my breath prayers/meditations involves:

> *a cleansing breath*
> *a centring breath*
> *a stilling breath*

all good things
Ted

Dear Ted:

TODAY IS DAY FOUR ON the Camino, and at the end of the long day today, after washing my clothes and having a shower, I painfully climbed the stairs to my third-floor room at the albergue in Uterga and found a young woman in tears at the top. Her companion was already comforting her, but it was enough to make me cry a little as I lay down on my bed. We were not the only people crying today. I saw others on the path and in the shower.

This is the fourth day. I have walked through the mountains, "become" a pilgrim, drunk more water in a day then I normally do in a month, fought with, lost, and made up with my daughter more than once, and have felt triumphant, more or less, at the end of each day simply for having arrived at a place of rest. I do feel stronger and surer with each step. Yesterday was a day of music. The day before I danced with the butterflies. The landscape has been idyllic, bucolic, perfect.

Today, though, was a day of pain, its ferocity utterly surprising. Malakai and I woke late in Pamplona and left quickly lest we be caught in the running of the bulls scheduled to begin today. It was not a happy morning, since neither of us are "morning people."

My husband wakes happily and whistles in the morning. It drives me crazy. I think I get my morning mood from my mother, and I have, in turn, passed it on to Malakai. My mother's sisters tell me that their nickname for her in childhood was "Bull."

When I was little, I never saw my mother in the morning. She ate the same thing for breakfast every day, in her room with the door shut. She ate two rectangles of Shredded Wheat in the special-offer rectangular blue Melmac Shredded Wheat dish that held them perfectly with milk. I never even saw her prepare this. She must have always gotten up early before retreating back to bed, or perhaps my father delivered it to her when he wasn't travelling on the road. My father was a travelling salesman.

I, too, ate the same thing every morning in the kitchen: white Wonder bread toast and brown sugar. My brother would eat Cheerios in a disgusting teenage-boy way with the milk dripping off his lips. I always had to put the plastic Cow Palace milk jug in between us so I couldn't see. These things linger, and my children are often amused by my inability to function in the morning – or to tolerate the eating of Cheerios in my presence.

Walking out of Pamplona was tedious. Tromping through suburbs, my mind would not focus. We left the hostel to enter streets littered with garbage and alcohol from the festivities of the night before. My pack was no lighter, despite all of my hopes and plans for Pamplona. My knees hurt.

As we finally came to the edge of town, heading out into the fields, I began your task with "Guide my Feet, Love." This quite quickly and surprisingly turned into the three-part yogic breath that begins in the abdomen, moves through the chest, reaches the throat, and ends with a strong exhale: Guide / My / Feet / Love, with the exhale on Love. That combination was so wonderful that by the time we were out of Pamplona, Malakai was far ahead and I was calm. It was fascinating because my pack is still too heavy, and yet for the first few hours this morning, I was light as air and happy. I could have walked all day like that. I have not experienced walking meditation before, but that is what it was.

Then, from within the calm, my thoughts moved on to other things, and I spent the rest of the day being forced to walk with my fear. That was a total surprise.

You know much about my fear of death because I met you at age fourteen, within a year of my mother's death. But you do not know anything about my fear of blindness, as it has been so long since we have spoken. These were the two things I carried with me today: the fear of blindness, and the fear of death.

In the summer when I was ten, my mother got sick. She had been dizzy a lot, which I knew because I was always with her. There were times in the early summer when we would be driving and she would have to pull over, resting her head on the steering wheel of her big blue Mercury Meteor. The Meteor had the same hideous wicker air freshener hanging from the cigarette lighter throughout my entire childhood. It had a horrible smell, unlike any other smell. I can smell it even now. I don't know how she could stand it.

The day she had her seizure, she was not feeling well and was lying down on the couch in the living room. She had a headache so I phoned my older sister Marlene to ask what to do. Marlene told me to get her a blanket and some juice, which I did. I sat on the recliner and we watched a soap opera; I think it was "The Edge of Night." I don't know what made me move, but she must have made a sound. I went to the couch and saw her shaking with her eyes rolled back and her face pastry-white. The sounds that she was making were not human sounds. I know that I kicked the coffee table out of the way, but I don't know why. Maybe it was because she was shaking so violently and I was worried that she would fall, but that is not what I remember. What I remember is the pitch and the wake of the centres of her deep brown eyes as they rolled, like a boat in a hurricane. I called my sister, screaming, and all I could get out was, "Mar! Mom!" Marlene told me to run and get the neighbours, and I did. I ran.

From that day until I was seventeen, I did not remember any of this. I only remembered what I had been told – the rest didn't exist.

You might remember that just before I left for Pakistan on Canada World Youth in 1986, I spent about six weeks in Winnipeg with you and the United Church youth-group gang. I was struggling with the idea of leaving home, and leaving my dad. I was only seventeen and yet I felt so responsible for so much. I can't remember whether I was in Winnipeg, or if I was somewhere else in Manitoba, on the day that I dreamt of my mother, but I fell asleep on someone's couch in the afternoon and slept deeply. I had a dream in which the entire sequence that I have just described flooded back, except that in my dream at the point where I kicked the coffee table out of the way, I was no longer ten, but seventeen, and my mother came out of the seizure. In my dream I sat on the couch and she put her head in my lap. She told me that my dad was a big boy and could take care of himself, that she and my dad loved me very much, and it was time for me to go. And then, in my dream, she closed her eyes, head resting in my lap, and died.

In reality, I was ten years old and I had to run for the neighbours, where I then stayed for the rest of that day and night after the ambulance came. I lost my mother that day. She was forty-nine. She didn't die until the day before she would have turned fifty-two, but she was never the same and began a slow, relentless decline. The only hope was at Christmas that year, after I had turned eleven, when she went to the Mayo Clinic and they found the brain tumour. I found out a couple of years ago, after my dad moved into long-term care, that he took out a mortgage on the house to pay for the surgery. The surgery removed most, but not all, of the tumour. And so she lived on until it grew back.

She started seeing snowflakes behind her eyes and heard bees buzzing. She wasn't able to play the piano. When told to wiggle her eyebrows, she flapped her arms. First she stopped being able to write a full sentence. Then she stopped being able to speak a full sentence. She stayed at home for the first year and I slept with her almost every night because she wanted me close. I picked her up off the floor when she fell in the night after an angiogram that made her horribly ill. I'm not sure why she, or anyone else, thought this was a good idea. But I slept with her, and she was warm.

Two of my aunts came to take care of us, one after the other. They both worked at the same racetrack in Windsor and so covered each other's shifts while the other was up in Thunder Bay for months at a time. Aunt Jeanine came first, and then Aunt Gerry. Aunt Pauline was often there, though she never stayed. She looks like me, or me like her. I love my aunts.

My mom wrote me two letters that I have at home in a yellowed Ziploc bag tucked in my underwear drawer. The first letter was a lie:

December, 1979

Hi Julie,
This has been a very busy week – with all kinds of Doctors – and lots of tests. Now that they are sure of what is wrong with me, I will have an operation on Monday. I have a small tumour on the left side in my head – where it hurt so much. The doctors will remove it then I should feel better in a couple of weeks. So don't worry, I'll soon feel a lot better.

Be good for Donna and Wayne – and have fun with the 2 (fluffys)

Lots of Love, Mom xxoo

She wrote the second one about three months later, and it was the truth:

March 13, 1980

Dearest Julie:

You are all going through a very bad time now because I am sick. I am sorry to put you through that. I don't understand why sickness like this happens either. But it does, to a lot of people.

We have to have faith and believe that it all happens for a good reason. Maybe to make all you kids and Dad stronger somehow. It is too bad all the kids do not use the church and praying to help them as you and dad do. But you don't have to go to church to be good, it just reminds you and makes it easier to be good. I have always loved you Julie and always will.

Love a whole lot,
Mommy.

When my mother finally was so sick that she had to be in the hospital, my aunts all left and I was moved to live with my sister Marlene. My mother was in the hospital for the last eighteen months of her life. She would wander. She walked out the front door of the hospital in her housecoat one day and got into a police car stopped at a red light, thinking it was a cab, waiting to take her home. She became paranoid, and marked her teddy bear so that the nurses wouldn't steal it. She hid behind furniture in the lounge or in the rooms of other patients. The nurses would sit her in the hall in her wheelchair and tie her to the railings so she wouldn't fall. She undid the knots and they called her "Houdini."

She had to be fed. Her brother, Johnny, came almost every day at lunch to feed her. My mother had forced Uncle Johnny into Alcoholics Anonymous, for reasons I will never know, but I think he had been a brutal man when drunk. He was a war hero but returned home to Hearst, Ontario, from a POW camp to find his first wife in bed with another man. The story is that he became very angry and spent some time in prison as a consequence. He drank from that point on. Uncle Johnny had no teeth, and I was always a bit afraid of him as a child. I didn't know him beyond my childhood because he died of a heart attack while my mother was still sick. My mother cried when he died: Uncle Johnny had fed my mother every day and he loved her — that much she knew. I think perhaps my mother taught Uncle Johnny the meaning of forgiveness. He had given my mother a small necklace and ring with a ruby inset. These things were given to me after she died, and somehow, along the way, I have lost both. I don't know how.

There were many people at the hospital suffering just as much as we were — we came to know them too, and they us. One elderly woman, whose husband was dying in the next room for many months, taught me how to crochet doll-dress toilet-paper holders. My dad still has one, bright yellow, on the back of his toilet at the nursing home. I often think of the kindness of that woman, who chose to pass the time in the family lounge teaching me to crochet and talking with me so gently. We crocheted red carnations too.

My mother slowly went blind and deaf. She stopped speaking. She didn't know us. She didn't know me. She couldn't see me. The last time I saw her was at Christmas, about five weeks before she died. I was thirteen by then. I put up a little "Precious Moments"

Christmas poster on the wall opposite her bed. She was wearing her blue housecoat and was slumped in a chair with her skinny legs poking out from the bottom. Her legs hadn't bloated in proportion to the rest of her. Her wig was on lopsided and it was old and worn. It had been a very long time since she had worn lipstick.

I can't remember if I kissed her or not. I don't think I did. She was beyond being recognizable as my mother by then, and we had been living for a year and a half with her gone from the house and gone from the world. When she was really dying, day after day for about a week in the middle of that last, cold January, I was left at home to babysit my nieces and nephews. I wasn't allowed to see her. No one would take me and I was too afraid to go alone. I could have gone by myself, simply by leaving school and taking a bus across town, but I was a good girl and would never have done that. My family thought that it would be too hard for me to see my mother as she was dying. Later, though, they didn't think it would be too hard for me to pack up all of her clothes by myself. My dad asked me to do this and no-one else was there. They didn't come to help me. That should never have been my job.

EVENTUALLY TODAY I HAD TO stop crying, because I was exhausted and the hill was too steep. I rested. It was then, while sitting, that I saw that the landscape surrounding me was full of wheat fields and sunflowers — much like Manitoba. I hadn't been paying attention. It was so beautiful and I took some pictures so that I can show you.

I rested at the bottom of a very large hill that climbs high above Pamplona and the surrounding farms. The ridge was lined with windmills, and the path ahead was visible as it wound up to where the windmills were. Malakai was far, far ahead, probably already at the top.

I procrastinated for a while, taking pictures of butterflies and flowers, but eventually I had to start the climb with my sore knees. I went back to "Guide my Feet, Love," and began to close my eyes. With the in-breath, – the Guide / My / Feet – I would close my eyes. And with the strong exhale – Love – I would open them. Walking half-blind, I started to breathe and say the second mantra you gave me, but I couldn't catch my stride. I couldn't catch my breath, and I started to cry again. So I had to move back to the three-part breath and keep going, eyes half open and half shut.

I am afraid of being blind, so I don't know why I kept closing my eyes. Three years ago I was diagnosed with uveitis and have super-duper specialists following my "condition," such as it is. Uveitis can be a precursor to all sorts of nasty things, quite apart from the danger it poses just on its own. There is the ever-present fear of a flare that will lead to blindness, and I have at least once woken to a darkened room that was growing slowly darker on the right side as the cells behind my iris exploded and covered the lens.

On that particular occasion, while in mid-flare I was required in two separate courts in two separate cities, something barely possible at the best of times. I was at the ophthalmologist's office the minute it opened and spent the remainder of that day trying to balance the reality of my immediate life with the expectations flooding me in spite of it. In the middle of trying to arrange for my court matters to be rescheduled, I was required by an opponent to provide a doctor's note – like a child in school. That was, perhaps, the beginning of a serious dissatisfaction with my present "milieu" that I have not yet vanquished.

I had spent many years wearing my abilities as a frenetic multi-tasker as a badge of honour, but on this day I was concerned only with saving my sight. I had specific instructions that in order to do this I must pound steroid drops into my eye every five minutes, without fail. Every five minutes, with the help of a small red egg timer, I had to turn my eye to the sky and put another drop in. This went on for four solid days and nights, without sleep.

I did what I was told, and I am not blind and still a lawyer, despite it all. I am also not crippled, which is a possibility for me. Depending on which specialist I talk to, there is a slight possibility that the reason my mother took so long to die was because it was not cancer, but rather neurosarcoidosis, of which uveitis can be a first sign. This tormented me for two years until my most recent specialist said, very kindly and firmly: "None of us knows what is coming for us. But you are my patient and I will treat you as it comes."

In other words, stop searching the Internet, stop finding new questions, and live.

And so, with every painful step I took today with my aching, tired body, I tried to work this through and give thanks to something – God, the universe, whatever it is that is bigger than me – for the fact that today I can see and I can move. It was hard. It was very hard to feel beyond the pain and the fear to a place of thanksgiving and gratitude.

In the afternoon, I was having trouble with my hip, which gives me some trouble anyway, and I felt weak as others passed me by on their rapid stride uphill. Obviously, I thought, they were not burdened with all of the problems I was struggling with. What an unfair thought. I'm sure that all of the people who passed me had their own burdens. But as they passed me, I was left with my small, limping, pained body and my thoughts jumbled, feeling the world striding forward past me.

I TRIED ALL OF YOUR MANTRAS again, without success, before settling on my own, which turned out to be this: Walk / Through / The / Pain. / Easy / Steps / Easy / Steps. With that, I burst. I poured rage and pain and tears into those words. The words became my only thoughts and they got me up the hill and over.

You gave me something that I needed today, and it marked a transition through the physical pain into something else altogether. It is something that I saw in the faces of others on the path, and in the tears of the woman in the hall. I heard somewhere that tears are poured into the stones of the Camino, and today I know that mine were. I watched my tears fall onto the ground as I walked, and I vividly remembered walking between my father and my brother, away from my mother's grave and watching their tears fall on either side of me in the snow.

You are one of the few people who knew how difficult it was for me at home in the years after my mother died. For some reason I sent you a story about my dad the day before I decided to match tasks to the alphabet for this walk. I wonder now if it was my email conversation with you on that Saturday, after so many years, that gave me the courage to do this. I think perhaps it was part of it. Thank you, Ted.

What I do know for sure, as I lie here writing to you in the late evening, is that this day is the beginning of understanding what is able to break through after these many steps. It's very similar to what I wrote about my dad, but in a different form. The story about my dad is about the power of music, which was the world I walked in yesterday, on my third day. It's also a bit about life as pilgrimage, I suppose. And the story, as you already know, is this:

My father has always been happiest when he is telling a good story. This trait has served him well all his life and serves him particularly well at age eighty-two in the nursing home where he lives, in the heart of the small village where I live.

My father's stories, freely given to all who will listen, now have the structure of a fugue – opening with the main theme and looping back in successive repetition. Small details are added. The main theme is repeated five times or more before the story is complete. This storytelling style is fuelled partly by vascular dementia and partly by the simple need to make sure the full story is heard and understood. Listening to one's parent as though one were listening to Bach requires a patience and an understanding that is rarely found in mid-life. But my father is persistent in the telling, and I am forced to be patient and to understand.

The most beautiful story is about a favourite teacher, long dead and invisible. I have scoured the Internet for any trace of Ford Rupert, who came from somewhere in the "south" to the Hearst Public School sometime in the 1930s. He stayed in Hearst for between two and ten years, depending on the day of my father's telling. I have heard this story more times than I can count and yet Ford Rupert does not appear to exist anywhere except in my father's memory.

Ford Rupert was most definitely a good man – or at least that is how my father remembers him. At the beginning of my father's last autumn of school, before he had to quit at age fourteen to go to the bush, Ford Rupert stood before the class and pulled out his violin. He played for the class without speaking. My father says that the class was silent in response. When Ford Rupert finished playing, then came the question: "How many of you want to learn to play the violin?" The entire class raised their hands.

Next came the task of convincing parents in the late 1930s, in Hearst, Ontario, to pay eight dollars each for violins ordered from the Eaton's Catalogue. The Eaton's catalogue was the only way to get anything in Hearst at that time. The pictures I have of my mother and her sisters in their catalogue clothes take my breath away — Franco-Ontarian beauties of the northern bush with a particular kind of sophistication that comes from knowing too much. Hearst came alive with goods from the Eaton's catalogue, and from the merchant — known only in my father's telling as "Willie the Jew" — who travelled from Whitby each summer with a truck full of oranges and peaches to exchange for moose hides and dandelion wine. My grandmother's dandelion wine fermented in the shadow of the dozens of birdhouses my ten-year-old father attached to the eaves of the old barn. He loved birds, and still does.

My father convinced his parents to buy the violin. I have no doubt that the violin was bought with the bootleg money that my grandfather earned, but there is a painful beauty in my father's telling of my grandfather lying on the couch in the kitchen after dinner every night saying "Play for me, Willy" until he slept....

Ford Rupert taught them to play, all of them — the Anglo-Protestant kids like my dad who went to school in the Orange Lodge before the school was built. The tension in these things is riveting.

I have now heard this story so many times that I can easily slip into nodding at my father and thinking about all of the things that I need to get back to doing after my quick visit. But if I do this, I miss the added details and the episodic nature of this fugue about Ford Rupert, and all of the others. Luckily for me, these things come up often, but I still think I must visit longer and listen better. My father, happy only for my company, says, "You are busy, come when you can." I pray that I grow to be half as graceful and kind as my father is.

Ford Rupert's class practised all through the fall and put on a Christmas concert for the town that drew a standing-room-only crowd. Of all of the stories about all of the nights of his life, my father is most proud of this. As he loses his memory to the point of sometimes not knowing what the lunch menu was, he remembers this night of the Christmas concert with crystal clarity. He is proud of many things, but he is very proud of this. All of the fathers came. Ford Rupert's class played "Ava Maria" for their parents, for Christmas. I still don't know when that was. Maybe it was 1939.

Thinking back to when I was very little, in about 1974, I can smell the closet in the basement of our house in Thunder Bay. It was at the corner of my father's workshop. He had a pegboard on which he let me paint the tracings of all of his tools, so he would know where to put them. To the left of the pegboard was the closet. It had a big barrel of ancient toys belonging to my older sisters and my brother. I was eight years younger than the last of them, and I did not play with those toys. It was a very mysterious closet. There was an old reel-to-reel tape recorder that still worked. An old phonograph. And an old violin. I remember asking my father about the violin, which I thought to be very beautiful and exotic. The only thing he told me then, in his mid-life, was that his parents had bought it for him when he was still in school.

The old phonograph, I now know, was used on the dock by the lake at midnight.

My father's fugue is beautiful. Its coda is this: we must age, both to know the significance of these things and to tell the story. There is no need to be afraid.

WHEN MY BROTHER DIED, AND I went to tell my father that he had lost his only son, I was not strong for him as I thought I should have been. I became a young child, sprawled across my dad's eighty-year-old lap, sobbing as he rubbed my head. I told him that I was supposed to be staying strong for him and he said: "It doesn't matter that I am old, I will always be your father."

Today, over two years later, I feel like I am emptying myself with so many tears. It is too hard. There will be nothing left of me if I keep this up, and yet I have none of the usual things to run to. I am so alone here, without my work and my family and my life to keep me busy and contained. Dear Ted — here in Uterga, I know that your words have spurred me on, yet again. I am so lucky. You need to know that I am truly blessed to have somehow picked you for this brutal, brutal day. I could not have walked through this day, with my thoughts flooding these hills, without having brought you with me. Truly.

Maybe for my dad there is no reason to be afraid. I know that he is not. But for me, I am so frightened about the rest. It hurts. I can't walk this far and think this much. I can't. Before I left, my dad told me not to walk on troubled water in Spain, but that is where I am. I spent this entire day mourning my mother, twenty-seven years too late and I'm still not ready.

The last thing you gave to me was this: "'Cause I don't want to run this race in vain." I have rested on that for a long time today. The temptation was to turn back and take a bus. But I didn't quit. I made it up that mountain and I am here in this place, resting. And so, just as you have suggested, I will try to put down my pen, take a cleansing breath, a centring breath, and a stilling breath … sleep … and carry on tomorrow. Ouch. Ouch. Gosh, Ted, it hurts. Did you know this was coming for me?

Love J.

5

YES, I WONDERED WHAT HAPPENED but I figured life got in the way. No big deal except it would have been good to reconnect if only for a few short hours. So now you need a favour, hey? Hmmmm. A task to focus on... Let's see....

Why don't you spend one of those twenty-six days looking at what life events have transpired to bring you to Spain walking the Camino Pilgrimage Route, why you're there and what you feel you want to find, discover and/or get out of your experience. Best of luck, e

LORCA, JULY 6, 2009

Dear Elvira:

IT HAS BEEN ALMOST A full year since I was in Victoria and didn't call as I had promised. I'm sorry. Life did get in the way. Life has been in the way for a very long time.

The easy answer to your question "What life events transpired to bring you to Spain" is this: I had most of July booked off. Malakai was in France and her July plans fell apart. She asked me to come to Europe, and I decided that I would, provided that we travelled cheaply and she used some of her summer money to pay for it. So here we are on the Camino, travelling for about twenty-five dollars a day, more or less.

That is the easy answer. The real answer is something quite different, and at the end of this horrible day I suppose I must thank you for forcing me, with your task, to think it through.

You don't know me as a lawyer – what a funny thought! But I am a lawyer, and in October 2008 I did a crazy thing. I got rid of all of my full-time staff, changed from regular business hours to "by appointment only," and made a pact with myself that I would leave white space in the calendar and spend July 2009 in the garden.

I have needed space desperately, and I have spent too many years surrounded by other people and their tragedies, their needs, their problems. I feel like a shadow. My eyes are constantly in-flamed from some heavy-duty autoimmune issues. I have been repeatedly on steroid eye drops and I am always, always tired. And bitchy. I have been very bitchy, most of the time.

How did that happen? You haven't seen me in years so this is perhaps a surprise – or not. I have been driven my whole life; I have never stopped moving. So in many ways, nothing has changed except that now, at age forty, I have been forced to catch up with myself and my bad genetic predispositions, and stare at the brick wall ahead of me.

Malakai has told me on this walk that there has always been crisis – and she is right. There has been a lot of stuff, some of which you know. The details don't matter, but life has definitely been heavy for a long time. On top of my personal life stuff, my successful practice has been both a source of pride and a chain. I have let myself fall into a trap of high overhead, high taxes, high stress, and far too much responsibility and anxiety over the lives of others. Some will say that this is a lawyer's life and the reason for the big pay cheque. That's partly true, I guess. But the Law Society is now spending a fortune studying why women are leaving the profession in droves. Fifty per cent of graduates are women, but only ten per cent are left after five years. Surprise, surprise.

There is a macho attitude in parts of this profession that only the strong survive, and that the strong are usually men who are not as "emotional." I disagree. I think it's just that there are some people, both men and women, who are more willing and able to completely check out of all of the other parts of themselves, for the rest of their lives. In fairness, there are a few happy lawyers who were simply born for the work and able to balance it beautifully — but that's not me. My body is now totally out of sync with my life.

Balance is difficult, in all things, and lawyers as a species are notorious for working inside the box, all of the time. This is something that you cannot understand until you experience it. It reminds me of something a young German girl said to me on the path the other day about not being able to know a need until you have had an experience. It's like that. When I was a tough little articling student, I laughed really hard at a magazine article advocating yoga for lawyers. Lawyers, said the article, are six times more likely than "normal" people to commit suicide, and yoga could help. I imagined my mentor, Marty, doing yoga. Marty was a huge, huge man. Standing on his head would not have been possible.

I thought the idea of yoga was very silly because, as you know, I completely rejected all flaky things after our university days. I found all the new-age stuff very, very silly — particularly after that woman told me, over coffee and cheesecake, that I had killed her in a past life. Maybe I did kill her in a past life, I don't know. I don't know anything about any of my past lives, so I suppose it's possible! But what am I supposed to do about it when I have all the stuff in *this* life to worry about? It is a concrete world, with real things to do, so get on with it. . . .

Needless to say, I have not incorporated yoga or past-life regression into my practice of law. I've done it the way others before me have done it. I've followed the rules and catered to the wishes of others. I've paid a lot of people to do things.

In my own practice (because it is my own practice) I have always had the freedom to do as I please. And yet I did not. I did not, in the beginning, spend one minute of time even thinking about what pleased me. On most days I worked long after my employees had left for the day. I catered to the whims and moods of my clients, who are almost always at a crisis point, a transition point, and are rarely calm.

I worked and worked to meet my own high expectations of myself. I fed on my success and good reputation and built a thriving, busy practice with two full-time staff, and a full-time student in the summer. Some days it was very fun and the fast pace produced adrenalin, which can be addictive – until there is no adrenalin left, because of course we have a finite supply. And it never fit particularly well, none of it. I was not a kid when I went to law school. I knew how to do other things, once upon a time. I have missed myself.

I quickly came to realize that I hate watching other people do things and I am not good at managing staff. In fact, I hate managing staff with a passion. But that's okay, because now I have no staff so I don't have to have anyone playing the role of employee. Except for Lisa, who comes in one day a week – but Lisa is not a legal assistant; she's a writer. It just so happens that she is also very funny and very good at filing.

I always worried far too much about being a bitch. I didn't want to be the bitch boss. But you know, a little distance goes a long way to shed all of the labels. Here, on the Camino, I can think to myself, "Yeah, so what?" And why is it that when men make the same demands, they are not called bitches? That's not right. I think men can be even bigger bitches than women. They are bitches in disguise.

I always tried to be generous and accommodating and not bitchy until I was well past the end of my rope – a typical girl. That was my problem. Maybe I should have be more bitchy from the start. Maybe I should have been bitchy the *whole* time. Who knows? It's hard to "be a man" when you are just not. Oh well, those days are done. I don't have to worry about strategic bitchiness any more. I am no longer in my "boss phase."

But on another note, you, who have known me for so long, are one of the few people who would best know the things I hoped to be able to hold true to – all of the ideas and ideals of my early adult life, steeped in learning and the early, uninhibited experience of new independence far from the world I grew up in. And I suppose, for the most part, I have indeed used my law degree to do some of the good I had hoped I would do. But there has been a great personal cost that was quite unexpected – and that, in a nutshell, is a big reason why I am here.

There are other reasons, entwined with the quiet desperation that has surprisingly given way to an open landscape around me in Spain. The white space in the calendar during the month of July was the result of a workshop I attended at a retreat in Massachusetts in October 2008 run by a Harvard-trained former corporate lawyer turned author. The title was *This Time I Dance*. I hadn't been dancing in a long time.

I knew I was going to this retreat for ten days in October.

What I didn't realize is that I would decide to get rid of all my staff the week before I left. I completely closed my office, changed my voicemail, turned on an automatic email reply, and bailed out. From the outside, if anyone had known I had done this, and in this way, it might have looked like I had lost my mind. But I hadn't. I had simply had enough.

On the first night at the retreat, I found myself sitting in the circle and introducing myself on command as though it were an AA meeting: "Hello, my name is Julie. I am a lawyer from Ontario. I have just gotten rid of my staff and locked my office and I don't know why I am here!" Over the next week, while figuring out why I was there, I met a number of very interesting, wonderful people. I did all of that United Church youth-group stuff when I was a teenager, but I hadn't been to a "retreat" in a long time. It surprised me that I fell right back into step with the trust and wide-openness that you can quickly develop with a group of strangers in that kind of environment. The kids think I've gone "woo woo." Can you believe it? How do I explain to them that I started out "woo woo?" I'm sure you appreciate what it's like to try to explain your pre-parent self to your adolescent children.

At the retreat, I made a friend named John, who is a second-generation Italian American, retired police officer, Vietnam vet, hostage negotiator, teacher, age sixty, and very tall. He and I hit it off immediately and spent three days talking and walking and sitting. At one point while walking, John stopped me with a shake and said: "What part of this don't you get? What do you think is going to happen if you let go of those plates you are spinning in the air? Guess what? They are going to keep spinning!"

John and I talked about all sorts of things that you would not normally talk about with "normal," everyday-life people. He told me about Vietnam. He talked about corruption and incompetence. He told me what it was like as a cop to shoot a man coming at him with a hatchet. Or to talk a woman off a bridge. He told me what it felt like to climb into a car at an accident scene to try unsuccessfully to save a teenage driver, only afterward realizing that there was a dead passenger in a prom-dress beneath his feet on the floor. He told me about what these things felt like. Really. John is not the sort of man who tells trophy-tales.

I told him about some things that stick to me, like the smell of the morgue or the room where they boil the bones. I took the train home from Toronto after leaving that place and I couldn't get the smell off me for hours. I hated the smell. I couldn't breathe. I also told John about watching an educational video of an autopsy in a room where every seat had a video monitor, in addition to the large video monitors hanging from the ceiling. It was like being on a trans-Atlantic flight, looking forward at dozens of television screens. Except these ones all showed the body of an old woman being eviscerated, and the screens were very, very close — without escape.

John has attended many autopsies, so we talked for a bit about that. We talked about how disturbing it is to see what the physical body turns into in seconds when a doctor who knows how to do this, and is allowed to do this, goes at the body with a saw and a knife. I am terrified of death. But I was a tough little chicken and I watched the whole thing while leaning as far back in my chair as I could to get away from the screen. Some of the men had to put their heads face down on the desk. I felt oddly triumphant about that.

At the time, I had remarked to someone that whatever had been in that human being on the screen was clearly gone, so there must be a soul or a heaven or something. By contrast, this person believed strongly that the slab of meat on the autopsy table in the video was all there was to it, simply the end. It made me sad. I didn't want to believe that, and my reaction suggested to me that I don't believe that at all. It was a leap of faith in that moment, because I disagreed so strongly.

Here is an interesting thing: at the same retreat, with John and me, there happened to be a pathologist who talked about how she loved her work, but hated office administration. She wanted to paint and she wanted to translate the beauty that she was able to see under the microscope into art. Death as art — imagine that! Or at least that is how I understood it, from where I was sitting. At the end of the retreat, I asked her to paint me something because she finds beautiful what I am most afraid of. Later she emailed me:

> To work on the idea I have I need to ask you what type of cancer scares you the most or what are you most afraid of dying from? I'm usually dealing with cancer at my job and that would be the easiest for me to get material to paint from. That will help me pick the image I will work from for the painting I'd like to do for you. Also, any images for you from nature (wildlife, plants or trees, etc.) that hold special significance for you would be helpful. I'm really excited to try this idea, but have been putting it off.

I have not yet been able to respond to her, but I will. When I am brave enough.

I told John some of my little stories in life, and when I talked about my mother, he cried. He felt so deeply for me something that I don't allow myself to feel.

Then, after spending so much time with John, I found myself at dinner one evening surrounded by women. You will understand that this is a situation that I seldom allow myself to be in

— sitting in a group of women, but there I was. One of the women was a comedian from Kansas, and she was indeed very funny. It was light and I enjoyed myself.

After dinner, one of the women — a photographer — asked if we would come to look at her work, which she had brought with her. Her work was beautiful: all photographs of pregnant women. We all shared stories and I found myself talking about the experience, after losing Alexander, of being told by a friend of a friend that at least I had been able to have a vaginal birth with him.

It was not a birth; it was a death — but that had appeared to be beside the point.

Why I decided to share this thing with these people — something that I do not share — is a mystery to me. But as I was telling the story, two things happened simultaneously. When I reached the point in the story where I said, "and then this horrible woman said… ," one of the women in the café said exactly the same words to me: "At least you were able to have a vaginal birth." It was a perfect mirror of the historical conversation that I was trying to put words to. At the same time as this was happening, the comedian from Kansas was standing behind me and she said, very softly, "Poor you."

I had to leave and cry long and hard in the Berkshire Mountains, alone. You will understand this, I know. I was angry. I rested again on the feeling that I hate women, capital "W," and especially wymyn, capital "Y," with all of the judgment and competition and girl bullshit. That's why I am never in a group of women. I hate it. That is what I thought as I retreated to my small dorm room and my bed.

To my surprise, I woke the next morning to a perfectly calm thought. I thought to myself, almost immediately upon waking, "Well, at least you were able to deliver him." And then I heard the voice from Kansas: "Poor you." Imagine that. I guess sometimes things need to repeat themselves until you have what you need.

After all of that yoga and talking and dancing (for there was dancing) at Kripalu, I rented a car and drove home. From that moment, spending July 2009 by myself in the garden was my goal. I had no clue — not even the beginning of an idea — that I would be here, writing to you, on the Camino. In my life, a year ago, this would have been an insane thought. Truly. I would have needed more permission than I ever could have garnered from my world as it then was.

Today, thinking of you and all of these things in answer to your task, I kept going backward in my thoughts until I was clawing my way up a hill in a rage — at what, I don't know. But constant physical struggle and exhaustion do appear to unlock some rather raw emotions after a few days, and today I felt rage, which I poured through my walking poles into the clay as I climbed higher. Today's landscape was ugly, not at all beautiful as it has been, and it was hard to walk through. It was also very hot.

My thoughts mirrored this as I traced my way behind the events of last October. Mingled with all of the work stuff are some other, deeper, layers of my little story. I know that. And I am really tired.

I GOT SICK IN 2006, WHEN I was thirty-seven. You do not know this. You will remember, I'm sure, that my brother became ill with a bizarre autoimmune illness in 1991, when he too was about thirty-seven. He was sick with inflamed internal organs for two years and then was in remission until his kidneys failed at age forty-five. He was on dialysis for five years until his kidney transplant in November 2006. He recovered at my house for about six weeks after the transplant before going back to Thunder Bay.

Then he got sick and died from a parasitic infection in March 2007, after a month on life support. What part of that is fair?

I didn't fly to Thunder Bay to see my brother on life support. I couldn't bear it, and I didn't want to be part of a wall of sisters at his deathbed. I couldn't bear that either. I am glad that my sisters were there. But I am also glad that I was not.

My brother bled into his catheters as the parasites did their invisible work. Hearing that was enough. I didn't want to see it. I wanted him here, in my house, as he was immediately after the transplant going back and forth to Toronto, singing to the Barenaked Ladies in the car. We went grocery shopping at Didi's — me with my ever-cluttered mind and him wearing his plaid pajama bottoms. We silently filled the cart, together, with all of the things that would have filled my mother's kitchen cupboards: Campbell's Tomato Soup, Sheriff's caramel spread, Wonder white bread. We laughed in the checkout line at what we had done. I miss him.

In July 2008, my sister wound up in intensive care with complete cardiac failure from sarcoidosis in her heart, the result of the same sort of autoimmune inflammation that had plagued my brother. I flew home for her because she was awake, she wanted me, and my nephew asked me to come. She survived and continues on with a heart that is working at thirty per cent. How much of one's self is required to keep living? Thirty per cent? Twenty per cent? Does the soul factor into these percentages?

For me, it's not my heart or my kidneys. It's my eyes. I don't want to dwell, but it does offer a particular perspective. This is the reason for seeking profound change and the reason for profound fear. Both are now ever present in me — and have not been very balanced. My right eye tends to be worse. My fear tends toward anger.

Tracing back, in May 2005, George was sick with acute pancreatitis and was hospitalized for a month. He was on a feeding tube and Demerol the whole time, and he didn't eat a thing for seven weeks. All four kids were still at home then. Stefan was sixteen. The girls were thirteen. Mary was eight. Stefan and the girls had their own teenage issues, all the way through all of this, and it is no wonder Malakai now tells me that life always felt like a crisis — because in those years, that's what it was. It was difficult all around.

With George, they were explicitly looking for pancreatic cancer, and for the first time ever I had no illusion of control over my adult life, something I have always struggled to maintain. At the hospital on a Saturday morning, our friends Peg and Mac came for a quick visit. As they were leaving, they emptied the contents of their trunk into mine in the hospital parking lot — a huge foil tray filled with two roast chickens and vegetables for an army. The kids and I ate for a solid week from that tray filled with their quiet care and help that I desperately needed, but couldn't ask for. Another dear friend cut our grass in the early morning before I was awake. These are the things that are never forgotten.

There was no cancer, obviously, because George is still alive. Pancreatic cancer or necrotizing pancreatitis both tend to gobble you up before you can blink. After many months it was discovered that the cause of those terrible weeks in hospital was a divided ductal system in George's pancreas. It's a tricky bit of business, but he has been worked on by specialists a couple of times, and for the most part he's just fine. In May of this year he trekked in Nepal for a month. We appear to be becoming a family of walkers, with our hair-trigger health.

George was sick in May 2005. By September of that same year, my dad was seventy-nine years old and suffering with gangrene in his foot and serious dementia. He ended up in Millbrook with me, and I soon knew he was not going home. He was hallucinating at night, with visions of people hanging from trees, rats on the floor, and fire in the windows. I had to fight with my sister, who thought and hoped that my dad was fine – not old, not on the edge of death, not sad. It was horrible. I have never felt such betrayal. And from her perspective, I think it may have felt that I was betraying her. It took two years for us to speak after I stole my dad from his home in Thunder Bay, but it's long done. My dad is still going strong, with good care and good medication. He doesn't see the rats anymore. He is full of grace.

The year before that, in July 2004, my mentor Marty died of cancer. I only began to appreciate how deeply that loss runs in me on my first day of walking here, through the Pyrenees.

Before that, from 2001 to 2004, it was all about being called to the Bar, building my practice, renovating the house, raising young children, dealing with the ex-spouses and other parents. Not easy, but it could have been worse. Definitely a busy time.

Before that, it was the Canadian Studies Master's degree (why I did that, I don't know), moving to Millbrook in the summer of 1997, George's dad dying that November, giving birth to Mary three weeks after his death, losing our baby Alexander in June 1998. I was still in law school, so I was back to it in September 1998. Dot one, carry on, and all of that.

Before that it was the undergraduate thesis and *The Peterborough Review*. Before that it was the struggle to keep my house and feed my baby, meeting George and blending our respective troubles in the middle of so much love. It has always been hard to balance the baggage, and we are not particularly good at it. But there is the true love part, so we soldier on doing the best we can – imperfect creatures that we are. The children sometimes judge us for our failures, but they are teenagers and what do they know? What do we know? It is what it is.

Before all of that, you were in my life, so there is no need to explain further.

As I was walking through one of the least picturesque parts of the Camino, there was a cemetery on my left and dry, scrub brush on my right. The cemetery was very creepy and crooked and I didn't want to look at it, so I looked down to my right and was in a very bad mood. I am not joking about the bad mood — I was in a hideously intense mood, full of rage and regret and emotions I can barely name.

I'm not sure what caught my eye exactly, but I saw something in the dirt and so went closer to look. I dug it out and it was the most beautiful snail shell, larger than what I would have expected to find on land. I dug around where I found the first, and there were many more. I formed a pile and then counted out twenty-seven. Down the path I found more, and I did pick some extras in case my precious shells break on the way to Santiago. I am carrying them in the top of my pack in the mesh bag that used to hold my underwear. That's the best I could do to protect them.

Today, as I dug my snails, I sat on the path in the dirt and cried a small river from the physical pain of the past five days and the sheer relief of being alone, being able to reflect on my own little history, being able to think and feel and be totally and completely alone in it. No wonder I am so tired. I realized today that these things don't happen on a short walk. It takes many, many steps and many, many thoughts. Your task has made me tell a story to myself and it has made me realize in some way that it is only that — a story, my story, for me. For me to have it, and feel it, and release it, I need to be alone.

There are always people out there who want to "share the pain," and while I think that I resist this, it seems that I always have someone in my life trying to play that role. I haven't been resisting it that hard, I guess. Maybe I have a small invisible light above my head, conveying the message "Please, please, share my pain. And then take it away." I don't think I have ever considered the importance of solitude in protecting myself from all of the stickiness. I am so glad that I was alone today with my little snail shells and my dirty fingernails on that stupid, horrible path. That is my lesson for today.

At one point, as I was trying to collect myself on the path, a Spanish man quietly passed me on the left and looked at me directly. He meant to look at me, and he said, "Paso por Paso." I didn't know what he was saying. I now know that he was saying, kindly, "Step by Step." This is the Camino.

Love J.

6

Dear Julie:

I THOUGHT VERY DEEPLY ABOUT THE task I would give to you for your incredible pilgrimage.

I spent some time travelling through Europe at eighteen … to "find myself." In many ways I did. But after travelling for long stretches alone I realized that what defined me in so many ways were the relationships and the people I encountered – long term relationships and short term too.

It is always important to have a solid place from which others understand who you are, such as your ethics, morals, and standards. But over time I have come to appreciate people however they are with flaws and gifts. My relationships, brief and long term have come to define who I am more than any other single factor in my life. I expect that many of your tasks might be reflective and self-analyzing and so....

— TASK —

JULIE, MY DEAR AND TREASURED friend, I would ask that you spend today away from yourself completely. Your task is to not speak at all of yourself today, not at all. No discussion of your husband or children, your work or friends. Today when you meet people I would like your engagement to be purely for the "other" – to be an active and intent listener – that you exist today to hear the stories of the others around you. Monks and nuns that I have known have a tremendous capacity for drawing conversation away from themselves to be completely present for the "other." The challenge is to keep the conversation going while never speaking of yourself. I ask that, if you can, you follow this after a day of quiet reflection / silence as I am sure you will have a task that requires this. The more people to converse with the better, of course. Please record if you are journaling at the end of your day, the stories told to you – the agonies, ecstasies as well as the mundane – your thoughts and experiences of not defining yourself for others and how they responded to you.

With Much Love

Felice

VILLAMAJOR DE MONJARDIN, JULY 7, 2009

Dear Felice:

TODAY I HAD SUCH A wonderful day – the walking was full of ease, and now all I want to do is sleep in the grass outside of this church where I am lying.

I made friends today and I consciously tried to do as you asked, offering only the most basic and minimal information about myself – my name is Julie and I am from Canada. However, this morning was quite funny because Malakai struck up a conversation with a man outside the albergue while she was waiting for me. It turns out that he is a Canadian from Thunder Bay, where I grew up, and indeed knows my sister Marlene very well. Amazing!

We left the albergue and Malakai went on ahead. I walked

alone for the first part of the day and I did have the thought that I would not meet or pass the time with anyone at all, for this is as it has been for the past two days. A solo journey. And an unhappy one at that. I have been truly miserable.

I caught up to a young Spanish couple, Galicians from Lugo. He is a teacher of laboratory medicine at the college in Lugo. His name is Miguel. She is either a doctor or a laboratory technician, I think the latter, and she works in a hospital near the sea. Her name is Oliva. She took English in school, and he is taking his Level One English now. They've been together for five years but are not married.

Oliva is an only child and will be responsible for caring for her parents as they age. Her mother, she says, "keeps her close," unlike Malakai and me, with Malakai charging so far ahead on her own. This is the way it is in Spain.

Miguel has a brother and a sister. He speaks Spanish and Galician. He explained the Pamplona Bull Run to me, which we only just missed by a day. The bulls run with the men in the street every day from July 5 to 15, to the bullfighting ring. It is usually the tourists who are maimed and hurt because they do not know what they are doing, he says.

I tried to explain what a moose is. I did not tell the story of walking, at the age of sixteen, with my boyfriend and his dog, and coming over a small rise to be face to face with a huge bull moose. We were immediately paralyzed, as was the dog. We watched the moose watch us, until it turned and sauntered into the bush. I consciously stopped myself from going on about my experiences with moose, and simply tried to concentrate on describing what they were. It was difficult, but I tried my best using a mix of Spanish and English, and mime and sand art. I also tried to explain what a beaver was. I made sure that they understood that we do not run after moose or beaver in Canada — that there was no parallel with the bull run. Can you imagine it? A moose run down Yonge Street.... Canadians would never be so careless, or so brave.

I also spent a very long time, in a round-about way, trying to explain the word "witch" — as in the witch-hunts that were common in the Basque Country and in Galicia in the medieval world. It was impossible for Oliva to understand what I was saying, though I tried for some time. Witches have become a favourite topic of mine. Talking of witches made me think about being a little girl and watching *Sesame Street* and *The Price is Right* every morning before I started to go to school. I loved *Sesame Street*, but I hated Day "W" because that was the day of "Wanda the Witch." Wanda scared me. I always needed my mother to watch with me on Day "W." I also hated "N" because I felt so sorry for "Ninny the Nincompoop."

Oliva and I compared cars and gas prices and the cost of houses and post-secondary education. In Spain, the government pays three thousand euros per year per student. Students live in residence and then move back home with their parents until marriage.

We discussed the various meanings of freedom — being mortgaged to the bank, being required by culture to care for aging parents, being expected by children to provide an inheritance, being allowed only two weeks of holidays per year and no siesta in the afternoon.

I can't remember all that we talked about, but I am happy to report that virtually none of it was about me. I didn't tell them how many other children I have, what my husband's name is, or what my life is like in specific terms. We talked about Canada and Spain, and all manner of universal life topics, all before Estella where we parted company so they could go to look at the church. I carried on and stopped at a grocery store where I bought cherries. I passed another "pilgrim" — a woman I had seen in the kitchen in the morning at the albergue. I offered her a cherry and continued on.

I came to a confusing bit of paved road where the direction of the Camino was not clearly marked, and an old Spanish man spoke to me, giving me many instructions in rapid Spanish. As I was trying to understand him, the woman I had offered a cherry to came up from behind and said, "Follow me, I know the way." I hadn't realized that she spoke English. She is Hungarian, trained as an engineer, but is now teaching English. She lives about an hour outside of Budapest with her husband, also an engineer. She has two children, ages twenty-four and twenty-six, the younger of whom will be finished school next year. They live together in a rented flat because home ownership is virtually impossible and, she says, Hungarian children are very skilled at remaining dependent for as long as they can.

I immediately liked her and did indeed listen carefully to her stories of the Camino, which she has walked alone many times. She asked me of my Camino experiences, and I told her only a small bit. I thought that since I had been asked a direct question about my present experience, it was only right that I should answer. She said, in response, "Just wait … it is the Camino … it is in the air … it is this."

I told her that we were going to have to take a train from Logrono to Leon to save time because we only have a month to walk. She convinced me that I must come back and walk alone the whole way, through the Meseta and past Santiago to Finisterre. Looking for topics other than myself, I told the Hungarian woman about Oliver Schroer. I let her hear a part of "Camino" on my iPhone and, to my surprise, she almost wept for the sadness of it. I don't hear it that way, but I was very moved by watching her face as she listened. There was something in the music that she understood, and I didn't.

We came to the famous wine fountain at Irache, the site of the only Camino webcam. Oliva and Miguel came soon afterward, and so I, with my new friends, waved to George on the webcam, and he texted me as I stood in front of the camera. What a world! I lost the Hungarian woman then, and have not seen her since.

The Spanish couple and I carried on, chatting in our mixed language and expression and signs to communicate the meanings we were trying to speak, all the way to where I am now — in the "albergue parroquial" in a small village called Villamajor de Monjarin. We have been rejoined by the couple from Thunder Bay, a woman from Ireland and her English / French boyfriend, an older couple from Holland — all of whom are now becoming familiar to me. We will leave them in Logrono in a couple of days because we must skip ahead, and I will be sad for that.

Up until dinner, I had hardly talked about myself at all, and have not been particularly important to the story of this day. Reading over your task again tonight, as I did this morning, this has indeed been a day about "others," following a long, hard day of solitude. You suggested to me that I should make sure that your task followed a day of reflection or silence, and what I realize is that very few of you who have given me tasks understood at the outset that I had assigned names to the letters of the alphabet, Day A through Day Z, twenty-six days in total. So the order was fixed, in fact, before I got the tasks. It is beginning to feel like I have very little choice about any of this, actually. What I do know is that I would not have been prepared for this place if I had not had my tasks to rest my thoughts on. That is a fact.

You wanted to know about my experience of not defining myself for others. It was truly a day that has been light and full of wonderful little surprises, like the chocolate bar Miguel handed to me as we walked into this town at the end of a long day. It was a hot day and I had thought that I would be leaving them here, where they were planning to stop, and continuing on to the next village, ten kilometres down the path where Malakai and I had agreed to meet. I was sad about this because it was such a wonderful day and I did not want the conversation to end. I have spent so much time alone so far; I did not want to be alone anymore. I was also very, very tired and so desperately wanted to stop walking.

As we rounded a corner on the path, Oliva noticed a piece of paper held down with two large rocks. It said, "Mommy, we are stopping here." I was overjoyed. We continued into the town, looking for the blue bandana. The bandana is now our sign: "This way mommy" or "here I am mommy." Malakai still calls me mommy, which I think is so sweet. I had better not tell her how much I like it or she will stop.

I was walking between my new friends when Miguel, to my right, quietly handed me the chocolate bar. Having no words to express my full body gratitude at such a gift, after twenty kilometres of walking, I could only make a huge kissy face and jump up and down.

When we got to the albergue, Malakai had left her blue bandana with a sandwich wrapped in it. She was asleep, I think. I washed my clothes and hers, as has become our habit, and hung them on the line in the churchyard. I then decided to get my towel and spread it on the ground to do yoga. I felt my straight strong back and quietly worked the knot out of my hip from the inside. I was all alone and not at all afflicted by anything. When I was done, I opened my eyes – clear, healthy eyes – and found a large group of people behind me, sitting on the stone wall, many of them watching me. I became immediately self-conscious, gathered myself, and left.

When i first started to do yoga, it was because I had read all sorts of things on the Internet about what uveitis can lead to. This was shortly after our dinner out with Nancy that February night in 2006 when I first felt the stab in my eye. Do you remember? I thought it was an ice chip because we were walking down Hunter Street through the snow to the restaurant. Why haven't we gone out to dinner since then? I know that it is entirely my fault, as I have ignored several invitations.

When I decided to learn yoga, I couldn't stand the idea of going to a yoga class full of flaky women. You know how strongly I feel about that! So I called Janette and asked her to come to the office three times per week at 4:00 p.m. to teach me — just me. My purpose in this was to end my work day early, like my staff, and to learn how to keep my back straight. I wanted to know how to prevent "bamboo spine" in case this was one of the things that might be coming for me.

Janette was wonderful and warm and taught me poses. After a few weeks, she came on a Friday afternoon and suggested that I lie down on my back to do a visualization exercise. At that point, I thought, "Oh, great, here we go! We're doing visualization now ... puh-lease!" I was not keen, but I really like Janette and I was grateful to her by then. And so I did what I was told.

Janette's voice was so smooth and she said so many things, I can't remember them all. But, at some point, I left myself. I don't know what happened or why it happened, but I was bathed in light that I felt pouring through my head. It grew in intensity and speed until I was simply being wrapped in swirling light, like a cocoon. Was this in my mind? Was it real? I have no clue. I know that at some point I heard Janette tell me to roll over into child's pose and then I heard the door shut as she left. I lay on the tile floor, in my conference room, in child's pose, and my spine began to vibrate and rock from side to side. I cried slow tears with metronome precision — one tear from the left, one tear from the right — right / left / right / left.

I'm not sure how long I stayed there, but when I got up I could barely move, so I called George to come and drive me around the corner from my office to home. George laughed, said he was making dinner, and told me that I could surely walk. I didn't tell him what had happened. I walked slowly home, and when I came through the door he looked at me and said, "What happened to you? You look like a baby bird!" I was. That was how I felt. I couldn't explain it, and the power of it was so frightening that I worried, in retrospect, about whether I was finally becoming unhinged.

The vibration in my spine has not stopped since. When I am doing yoga, or going to sleep, my spine rocks like a boat. My spine tingles and floods across my back when certain people come near me. Sometimes it feels like it's moving in a circle. Sometimes it's straight up and down. It's always the same base feeling, regardless of the strength or the spread. The vibration is very, very strong when I am quiet, and never more so than on the Camino where I have felt positively resonant. That is the only word I can find to describe my imperfect spine: perfectly resonant.

When I was last in Massachusetts with my neighbour Sue, as we were leaving to head home we happened to turn left instead of right (I think because I wanted to go right and Sue said to go left). We discovered Tanglewood and the Boston Symphony summer concert of the *Marriage of Figaro*, just around the corner from Kripalu. Of course we stopped and therefore didn't get home until the early morning of the next day. At Tanglewood, while lying on the grass and listening to opera, which I had hated before that moment, I felt my spine intensely and felt as though I was tunnelling through the grass to the centre of the earth. I think I quietly told Sue about this sensation, hoping she wouldn't think that I was completely nuts. I can't remember if I really did say it out loud. I have told very few people about this, before now. I don't believe in the flaky stuff, remember?

Later on, I stopped doing yoga as often because the vibration was getting so strong that it was scaring me. I had also done yoga one night in the sunroom, and the moon outside the window was bright and full. I felt so pulled, and so grateful, and so powerful. I worried about being pulled so. I did not want to be pulled right out of my life. I also did not want to be having experiences that I couldn't talk about.

So I stopped doing yoga and then got myself going in an inner loop that led me to decide that the vibration in my spine must be connected to a neurological disorder. I read up on neurosarcoidosis, which is often preceded by uveitis by about four years. I'm almost there, I have thought. None of the specialists have confirmed this, obviously, although it is a possibility. I have been afraid of this on so many levels — more than I can tell you.

I had a difficult time sleeping this afternoon in this albergue, which is run by the most gracious and lovely *hospitaliero*. It consists only of mattresses on a wooden platform and some bunk beds. No sheets and no pillows. I have been sleeping in my lovely silk cocoon, which I have come to treasure. Tonight I will sleep with my head at the opposite end of the bed from the people sleeping beside me in a long row. I prefer to sleep with their feet, for some reason. It is all a bit dank, as we have all been on the road for the better part of a week now. There are showers and the daily washing of clothes, but still all of the shoes must stay outside or it would be unbearable.

The girl at Mountain Equipment Co-op, where I bought all my stuff, said that the silk cocoon keeps the bed bugs from biting, but I think I have lice. God, I hope I don't have lice. Do you remember when all of our kids had lice and we had to declare a universal lice-cleaning day with the "other parents," resulting in endless stupid discussions about the inherent dangers of lice shampoo and whether we could use it on the kids without court order, or something to that effect? There were granddaddy lice running around our house, and using the toxic shampoo was just fine with me. I don't think the children have suffered from it — at least not yet. If I have lice now, I'll have to find some of the toxic shampoo here in Spain, I guess.

For some reason, the top section of my pack is full of all of my special and hidden things that I very much want to carry: your mother's rosary, Sufi prayer beads from Iraq, some stones for the huge pile at the Cruz de Ferro, a black bear claw complete with the fur and tobacco that came with this gift, and a pile of snail shells that I dug up yesterday and tucked away in my mesh underwear bag.

Oh Felice, I did find today difficult, narcissist that I am, but setting myself aside was much needed and your task came on the perfect day. You also must know that I wore your mother's rosary all day. It made a beautiful sound as I walked. On my ninth day, I have been given a task that requires a rosary, so I will wear it then and use the instructions you gave me. I will also wear it into Santiago and into the cathedral for the pilgrims' mass. When I am not wearing it, it is in the top of my pack with the bear claw. I've kept it inside its precious gold box, and I am trying to take good care of that too.

To be so entrusted with something so precious for my journey has forced me not to discount this as frivolous. I have not discounted my thoughts. I am listening. For that, I am very grateful.

Love J.

7

Dear Julie:

"LISTEN TO THE WIND" — this phrase haunts me.

I was thinking of you and this beautiful, difficult walk you are going to take and your lovely inclusion of your friends — so ... an idea.

If you could take time — a minute, minutes of stillness and "listen to the wind" of the place, the day, or your heart or your head — and find a word — one word each day — that expresses the message that you hear, you would end up with twenty-six words that would embrace each day — each different and each in any language that seems to encompass the particular message of that day, that moment

My love,

Grace

P.S. Julie — didn't know there was anything on the back of this paper when I wrote on the other side — then found, alas... this — so I thought maybe it was to be — so I boxed the verbs and that made a strange sense.

Seek; Find; Develop; Prepare; Submit; Put; Deliver; Take; Join; Check; Have; Bring; LOVE

Dear Grace:

YOUR TASK IS ONE THAT has spilled over to each day from the start, but today was my day of wind. You have specifically tasked me to think about the messages in the wind, and indeed I have been trying to listen.

It's interesting to me that you describe feeling "haunted" by the phrase. I often feel haunted, or pulled – it is a difficult feeling to describe.

Three days ago, I climbed to the top of the hill with the windmills and down again on a very difficult and hot day full of tears. This was the same day of early tromping through wheat fields, and at one moment I had to stop, truly, and listen to the sound of the rustling wheat. This was not because of your task, because it was not your day, but once I had stopped, my mind immediately turned to you. The sound of the wheat was enormous and stretched far across the fields.

Later on that day, I looked up just as the wind lifted cut wheat, golden and light, off the top of the field and spun it about ten feet above the ground ahead of me on the path. It shimmered gold and it danced, the way butterflies have danced each day, all through the Camino. It was beautiful.

I have a picture of a wheat field looking down from the ridge. There is a distinct pattern in the wheat, and I wondered about the phenomenon of crop circles, and wind as a transformative and energetic force.

A butterfly flaps its wings as it dances the organizing metaphor of quantum chaos. I love the notion of quantum chaos and the theory that the motion of a butterfly's wings can create the tiniest of changes in the atmosphere that could alter the course of a tornado. The butterfly doesn't think this through – it simply dances in the wind.

This makes me think of something that was said to me in February by a woman, an elder, whom I have known for almost as long as I have known you but have seen only three times. She gave me a hawk feather when I was twenty-five. One day I lost it – it had always been hanging from the ceiling and then it was gone. After not speaking to her for fifteen years, I had a need to find her and was very oddly encouraged to do so by a retired police officer who works part-time in the Superior Court, escorting the judge from chambers to courtroom. His name is Herb. The day after I returned from my brother's funeral, in the middle of a busy court day, Herb whispered his condolences and asked me a question which, in a round-about way, was this: "What animal did your brother send you and do you have an elder?" It was a shocking question from Herb, entirely out of the usual context of our interactions, and my immediate response, without hesitation was, more or less, "My brother sent me a deer and yes, her name is Proud Woman." I said this out loud, without thinking first. I was instantly afraid. Herb then told me that I had better find her.

I couldn't remember her real name. She lived in a small town in Northern Ontario, where I had last visited her on my way back north to visit my family. Later in the day, after sitting at my desk for a long time, staring blankly at my computer full of work, I looked up the General Store in the place where I thought she lived and called. I told the store clerk that I was looking for a woman who lived there who called herself Proud Woman. The woman at the other end of the phone laughed and said, "You mean the witch?" Without thinking, I said, "Yes – that's her." She had moved, I was told, to live with her son. I found her phone number and called. The conversation began with me saying that I didn't think she would remember me but I was glad to have found her. She did remember me, appeared to find my call quite amusing, and said that she had always known that I would find her.

That was April 2007. Proud Woman told me to finish "doing whatever I was doing" and then come. I said that I would call the following week, and she laughed. I meant it – I didn't think I had that much I had to do. But time went on and I didn't call. Months went by. I often saw Herb at court and, from time to time, he would gently and quietly prod me with another question: "Have you gone to see that woman yet?"

About a year later, on the occasion of the swearing-in of a colleague who had been appointed to the bench, Herb asked me again and told me that I had better not wait too long. After that, I tried to call Proud Woman many times, but the phone was never answered and my messages weren't returned. I became convinced that she had died and I was angry with myself for being too busy and too afraid to make the time to go.

But then, in February 2009, I was in the law library making arrangements to travel for an entirely different reason to the town where Proud Woman lived. I was paged into court and ran downstairs to answer the page. On my way back, I ran into Herb, my circumstantial guide, and he said that I really might want to get in touch with "that woman." I threw up my hands, went back to the law library, picked up the phone, and called. Proud Woman answered immediately and asked me when I was coming. She knew.

When I finally saw her this past February, I only sat and listened. She talked and talked and told me many, many things. I will not repeat them now, but important to the notion of the butterfly's wings and the wind is something she said to me about bears and seeds. I told Proud Woman that I had lost the hawk feather she had given me and that I was upset with myself for this. Again her response was laughter, along with the suggestion that I didn't need that anymore. She gave me a black bear claw, complete with fur and wrapped in tobacco.

The next time I saw Herb at court, I had to sneak him away into the very small cell where prisoners are kept during jury trials, so that I could show him my claw. For some reason, on that day, in the cell, Herb and I also talked about whales.

It is true that the medicine comes first and the journey follows.

Proud Woman told me that a bear runs through the forest gathering seeds on its coat. The seeds are caught by the fur in one place and fall to the ground somewhere else, as the bear goes on his way. The bear gives no thought to the seeds or where the seeds will land or what will become of them. Its coat is too slick. It's similar to the butterfly wings, isn't it? And the wind?

Proud Woman told me about a time when she was young and was taken into the bush by an elder. She said that as they sat by the river at night, the ends of all of the branches of all of the bushes lit up like a Christmas tree.

She also gave me a stone, which I was told to place in moving water. When I visited Malakai in British Columbia in early March, I threw the stone into the Pacific Ocean. As you know, I was obsessed with whales at that point, and so I had the thought that I was throwing a piece of my soul to the whales. We can turn anything into a symbol, can't we? We make things so complicated. But that is what I did.

I have carried my bear claw in my purse since the day Proud Woman gave it to me, and I am carrying it in my pack now — no one knows this, of course. These are not things I can talk about easily, my life being what it is. The claw is now separated from the fur because Proud Woman had said that I might want to wear it around my neck someday. Before leaving for Spain I decided that I well might. It was difficult to think about how this would be possible, and so, of course, I asked Glenn to try to figure it out.

In my experience, there is nothing that can't be figured out in Glenn's shop. One day, after three hours driving home from somewhere in horrible traffic with my thoughts raging at the injustice of that particular day, I drove into the dark village and saw the shop lights on. I knew that it would be Donny who was there building his musical instruments, and I stopped to ask one question — a very childish and innocent question: "What do you do to be able to be in the world when the world is so wrong?"

Donny, of course, didn't have the answer, but he is a quietly brilliant and kind man, and he gave me the space to cry just a little before going home. He had no idea what exactly it was that I was crying about, nor does he know how very important those few minutes were. I don't think he would particularly care. Donny's coat is slick.

Glenn was not sure what to do about the bear claw, but I told him that it could not be touched by anyone but him. I don't know why I felt that so strongly, but I did. Glenn spent a great deal of time carefully removing the claw from the fur and deciding how the hole in the top should be precisely placed. When he gave it back to me, he explained that it would require a leather thong, and showed me how to cut an imaginary piece of leather on an angle so it would thread through properly. I meant to find the leather at a tack shop, but I didn't have time. I asked George to do it, but he forgot. So I am not wearing my claw — I am carrying it in the top of my pack, and hoping that I will be able to buy some leather in Logrono.

As for the wind.... Daily, in the heat of the afternoon, I search for the wind and will often stop to turn my face to it. I have never had the occasion to yearn for it so, but in the endless walking, things have become much more simple. My days have now fallen into the routine of this form of life. I passed a couple from Holland today. They are both perhaps sixty and were sitting quietly on a bench. I have seen them many times since Roncesvalles, and today the man smiled and said, as I passed, "There is no better life than the life of a pilgrim!"

A couple of days ago, I might have become angry at this thought, might have considered it a silly, scripted phrase, and pounded my poles into the dust as I have done now up many despised hills. I have not wanted to be "a pilgrim." Pilgrimage is for people who are serious and slightly sanctimonious, not for people like me who just walk up stupid, dusty hills because they had a stupid idea to come here and just can't give up and go home. I have never quit anything in my life. So I can't quit this.

But today I am softer and have turned a corner. I feel that I have settled in; my shoes are not hurting, my legs are stronger. I have the rhythm of my walking poles and several small internal songs to carry me — some given to me with earlier tasks, some from my childhood, and some I have simply made up. Sometimes I sing out loud, to no one and only when no one is watching.

My routine is now fixed. I know when and how to get up without disturbing others. I know how to be thankful in Spanish. I know how long it takes for my clothes to dry, both inside and outside, and can now decide whether I need to wash my clothes before I nap, depending on the time of my arrival at the next albergue. I also know how to discreetly position my underwear on the back of my pack in the morning if they are still damp, so they will dry by lunchtime. I only have two pairs of underwear, so this is very important.

My pack is becoming lighter on my back, even though I have not shipped anything home yet. I will do that in Logrono.

I have spent two full days walking with new friends, with little common language, and we have succeeded in discussing the full range of life's topics with simple words, expressions, gestures, and drawings in the dirt with the end of a walking pole. Today we talked about the vibrations in the whale's song, a topic that you and I have discussed, so you will appreciate how difficult it was to convey what I was attempting to say about my thoughts on the subject.

Not long after you and I spoke of this, I talked at length about the whales with an elderly client. She had much to say on the topic, and when she returned to my office on Valentine's Day, she brought me a present and a note. She told me that she had brought me chocolates for Valentine's Day and left. When I opened the package it was not chocolate at all. It was a beautiful book about whales.

During that same visit to the office, my client was very encouraging to Lisa (my very part-time assistant, who is a writer in real life) about her next book, which is called *With Her Boots On*. The woman said, "Just like a good soldier." This made me laugh then, and I have thought about it each day on the Camino as I try to measure my steps. Isn't it interesting, the gifts that we give to each other? It's all about the butterflies and the bears. It is important to remain slick, not sticky, so that things can fall as they should.

Today I felt great happiness and warmth in the company of some new friends. A couple of Americans joined us at one point and we discussed, in English, where we are from and "what we do" – nothing more. Afterward, I told Oliva and Miguel that I appear to be able to communicate more deeply without my own language to trap me. I have found that to be very interesting. I write my letters every night and struggle to find the words to respond to my tasks and my days here. This place has no language. It is like the wind. One must listen very carefully, in very many ways.

Oliva, Miguel, and I have smiled and appreciated the old gossiping men sitting at the *fuente* (fountain) of each small town we've walked through. They sit and keep track of pilgrims — just as all of the men at the Millbrook Family Restaurant would do if we had such a path. Day after day, year after year, I imagine. They are very funny, and very encouraging, which one can only know if you either speak Spanish or are walking with a Spanish friend.

It is not the pilgrimage to Santiago itself that moves most of the travellers — and after several days of walking, it is no longer the *idea* of pilgrimage that is important. I thought about this today and realized that all of this must start with one thought, one idea: I will do the Camino. For whatever reason — to "walk in the wilderness," to "walk the Way of St. James," to succeed in the physical challenge, to beat the other pilgrims to the next albergue, to say at home "I did this; look at my pictures," to escape.

This afternoon, as I watched a Spanish pilgrim, trained as a nurse, tend to the dangerous blisters of a twenty-two-year-old Colorado boy on the bench in the sun, I pondered how all of these ideas and thoughts become completely subsumed by the very real experience of pilgrimage — simply walking in one direction, toward something. It doesn't even matter what you are walking toward anymore. It is simply the act and pain of moving in one direction for a very long time.

The boy from Colorado had, in his words, met up with some "crazy Basque dudes" and had walked forty kilometres per day for three days in a row. His body has now shown him limits that his mind did not know. It is a profound lesson and one that may be lost on him until much later in life.

My experience has been quite the opposite. Without blisters

and with my body strengthening and healthy, I find that my mind is pushing my body beyond the physical limits that I thought I had. I am also older, and have a bit more of myself to walk through.

Malakai and I have fallen into a quiet, simple routine, which is the one thing that has not been negotiated and fought about between us — it is just there. She races on ahead with her strong body and leaves her blue bandana on the path where I am to meet her at the next albergue. She is usually sleeping when I arrive; often she has bought food for me, which is waiting, and I take her clothes while she sleeps and wash them. It is a daily act of love on my part, and I hope that at the end of this month of ours she will know that. I know that the fruit that she leaves for me in her blue bandana, while she naps, is love.

This morning at the wonderful but stinky albergue, the *hospitaliero* and his wife made coffee and played a CD with Pachelbel's Canon, the "Air on a G-string," and "Jesu, Joy of Man's Desiring." These are three of my favourite classical pieces and, by coincidence, I downloaded the sheet music for all three from the Internet not long before coming to Spain. Before I left I had not been playing the piano. I had not had time.

I first learned to play the piano with my mother, who had herself returned to music in her forties. When she died, I stopped playing. I started again when the children began taking lessons from Dorinda. I began lessons too. There was a song that my mother used to play and that I had learned — it is an obscure little Sonatina by Clementi and I have not heard it anywhere else. One evening when I was playing one of my practice pieces for Dorinda, she pushed me out of the way and slid onto the piano bench, as she sometimes did, and said, "No, like this!" She started to play my mother's Sonatina. How did she know?

In the morning in the albergue, the music was quiet and beautiful, the coffee was delicious, and there were a lot of flies. The whispers and rustling are now familiar and comforting, with the added pleasure that some of these people that I ate with I have now come to know.

There is a lovely Irish girl named Fionnuala, a raven-haired beauty from Donegal with lily-white skin. She is about to begin her first teaching job – I think she teaches biology and chemistry. She is travelling with her boyfriend who is British and lives in the south of France. He has been travelling in Spain for a year, I think. I can't remember. He's moving to Dublin to go back to school – and presumably to be with Fionnuala.

Fionnuala's name means "white-shouldered," and her skin is so lily-white that the Spanish women talk about her as she passes. The black Irish, with raven hair and dark eyes like George, are apparently the product of some ancient commingling of the Celts and Spanish Moors. Fionnuala has even been mentioned by others along the way, because she is truly lovely. I joked with her that in medieval times she would have surely become "Fionnuala, Swan Goddess of the Camino," because of the way that her reputation precedes her and the attention she draws from the local women when she arrives.

Tonight, at dinner, there was a new choice in the pilgrims' menu that has become our staple diet and has, until now, consisted of fatty beef stew, bread, and a large bottle of Spanish wine. Tonight there was salmon, wine, and excellent company: an Austrian couple, a German man and his son, two Basque separatist primary-school teachers (the crazy Basque dudes, as it turns out), two Québécois teachers, a Belgian mother and daughter, and an vegan English music teacher living in Dubai. A motley crew and much fun, with many bits and pieces of language and laughter.

I am more expressive with these people because it is necessary, and I feel myself coming alive. There was a young Danish girl in the washroom tonight who wished to counsel me regarding the need for intense training before embarking on the Camino, and I could not help but laugh out loud while brushing my teeth. I had to tell her that I decided three weeks ago to come and start walking – and that's it. The young girl immediately lost interest in me, and I hope she didn't think I was laughing at her. I was laughing at myself for thinking I could just up and walk twenty-five kilometres a day with a pack I had never before carried. Perhaps if I had trained better I would not have cried through so many of the past days and would be much more organized about processing my rangy emotions.

The Danish girl moved along to organize her small impromptu group for the next day – deciding on the time of departure from the albergue (between 6:00 and 6:30 a.m., closer to 6:10, she thought) and the point of entry upon the various monuments along the next day's route. There will always be people who, for their own reasons at various stages in life, will need to create a uniform experience around them. It is a need to synchronize all of the left brains of all of the people – an impossible task.

Almost everyone in this room is scribbling in a journal – private thoughts that somehow are made more real by putting pen to paper. The need to communicate is a universal need – to share a story, a feeling, an expanded world. The expanded world is an endless synchronicity without effort, and something that occurs far above the details of the day.

In my conversations here, as with every conversation I have ever had with you, I feel connected to a universal quest – by a yearning, a word, a vibration, a note. This impulse can only do good, or be good, if I let myself align with what I yearn for. That is what you have brought and sustained in my life, Grace. Thank you.

The majority of my time is spent with people with whom I would never share these things, and people who are rarely truly happy to see me. I spend so much time in a courtroom, not in my garden. I spend a lot of my time with unhappy people, in unhappy places, and I have become unhappy. Nothing grows in a court-room. I should not be there. It's not about being tough enough (puffy-tough), or "having what it takes," or all of that ridiculous man-talk. I should just remember that I am soft enough to know that there are other things to this life. I should remember that it is okay to be happy. It is okay to be healthy. I should remember that it is okay to walk, and think, and be more than all of the pettiness of the "big-man" world.

I was thinking about the first time I met you just before I was pregnant with Malakai. Harald sold me that first computer on which I later coded Evelyn's recipes for *Today's Parent* to pay the bills. I was at your house so that Harald could show me how it worked. That was long before my Millbrook life and my law life. What a funny world it is, because there you are, and here I am.

Back then at our first meeting, I was twenty-two years old – an age that Malakai has told me several times on the walk was far too young to be doing anything that I was doing at the time. Do you remember that by the time I spoke to you next, I was in fact pregnant and told you that I had considered the name Grace if the baby was a girl? I love the name Grace. And I loved you from the first moment. You were cutting a loaf of beautiful dense bread on the cutting board in your kitchen, and you gently suggested to Harald that he need not spend so much time explaining the inner workings of the computer to me. I knew true beauty when I encountered it, and my experience of you in the eighteen years since has shown this to be more than true. Lucky me that you have been in my life for so long. You are, perhaps, the centre of the web.

Tonight as I sat and re-read your task, I considered the agenda for your beautiful community garden and I tried to write my own little agenda for this journey, without thinking it through. I closed my eyes and wrote words as though they were delivered by the wind. Here is what I wrote:

Prepare the mind
Submit the will
Put childish things away
Deliver thoughts and words
Take heart
Join others
Check your fear at the door
Have a coffee
Bring your love

I must ask you why, when circling the verbs on the Community Garden Agenda, you added in LOVE. It must have been the wind.

I didn't name my baby Grace, obviously. But today, my task from you is a word for this day, and it is clear, in all of its many, many meanings. It was riding on the wings of the butterflies, and it was my experience of this day. The word for today came to me on a windy hill as I blew my love for you with my breath, hoping that it would travel far:

Grace.

Love J.

P.S. Here are my daily words matched to the tasks, places and people of each day:

— A —

Propel

make me a channel of your peace

Roncesvalles

Mary-Anne

— B —

Patience

the millions who have travelled this path

Zubiri

Barbara

— C —

Divest

one space, one colour, one note

Pamplona

Agda

— D —

Breathe

guide my feet, Love

Uterga

Ted

— E —

Step

life got in the way

Lorca

Elvira

— F —

Laugh

you exist today to hear

Villamayor de Monjardin

Felice

— G —

Grace

listen to the wind

Torres del Rio

Grace

— H —

Power

par coeur

Logrono

Dominic & George

— I —

Ease

pray

Astorga

Betty

— J —

Spill

you have enormous talent, you must not waste it

Rabanal del Camino

Jim

— K —

Wonder

immerse yourself in a litany and catalogue of self-love

Manjarin

Tama

— L —

Exhale

at the end of the day list five things you are most grateful for

Ponferrada

Fran

— M —

Loss

examine why and how you fail to identify those who will hurt you

Villafranca del Bierzo

Meredith

— N —

Courage

if I did not hold these fears, what would I be doing?

La Faba

Brian

— O —

Sleep

discover the hidden seed

Triacastela

Lisa

— P —

Solitude

capture Cerberus, the three headed dog of Hades

Sarria

Peg

— Q —

Humanity

visualize world peace

Portomarin

Glenn

— R —

Encouragement

observe windows

Palas de Rei

Ross

— S —

Lost

look up

Arzua

Sylvia

— T —

Oooommmm

be mellow

Santiago

Janette

—U—

Fiddle

think about nothing

Santiago

Suzan

—V—

Growl

be an animal

Santiago

Evelyn

—W—

Blue

think of your adventure as colour

Finisterre

Joe & Murielle

—X—

Footprints

create something with Malakai

Finisterre

Sue

—Y—

Release

give something away

Santiago

Nancy

— z —

Wish

make a list

Santiago

Garth

8

Dear Julie:

I MOST CERTAINLY DID — I'M honoured to be among those you asked. I went off and listened to excerpts of Oliver Schroer while trying to think — and sent a copy of that album to a friend in need here in Montreal. So I have been thinking of what I could set as a task — but you should know that your announcement has already caused music about the Camino to be given to someone — and I carry this request as a meditation....

The task I offer you is this: to say out loud, on the crest of a hill, a poem, favoured passage, song — by heart. To say by heart — it's the same in French, *par cœur* — it's as though we are invited to know that memory is somewhere else within us, with us, beyond the mind. Or that the heart, the sense of love, is in all memory.
Many blessings for your journey
Dominic

[from George]

Dear Julie, *Task "H" (for husband — you didn't ask, but you mentioned it)*
OK — HERE'S A SIMPLE one. Use this as your mantra all day.
Make sure it's a hard walking day and carefully consider each line.

> The Lord is my Shepherd; I shall not want.
> He maketh me to lie down in green pastures:
> He leadeth me beside the still waters.
> He restoreth my soul:
> He leadeth me in the paths of righteousness for His
>   name's sake
> Yea, though I walk through the valley of the shadow of death,
>   I will fear no evil: For thou art with me; Thy rod and thy
>   staff, they comfort me.
> Thou preparest a table before me in the presence of mine
>   enemies; Thou anointest my head with oil; My cup
>   runneth over.
> Surely goodness and mercy shall follow me all the days of my
>   life, and I will dwell in the House of the Lord forever.

xoxox G.

LOGRONO, JULY 9, 2009

Dear Dominic & George:

I'M NOT SURE IF I should write one or two letters today. I
think I will write one, to be sent to two places, but that might
prove to be difficult.

    I can't remember when I told George that I was doing this —
I think it may have been after Joe sent his response to George's
email address. I was worried that he would think I was being silly.
Funny the things that we try to hide from those who know us the

best. When he asked, I said something like ha, ha, I left "H" open for husband – not thinking he would ever take me seriously.

And so when I received an email from George, giving me a task for "H," I immediately thought: "Oh shit, Dominic has H!" It was only, of course, after reading the two tasks together that the perfect coherence in it was apparent to me.

The intimacy of marriage is sometimes painful. Raising children is sometimes painful. Watching your parents die or prepare for death, is painful. I didn't ask for any of that to be in my task list. But it would appear that you get what you need, not what you ask for. "H" is therefore a shared day, and obviously George doesn't think I'm all that silly.

IT IS ALSO NO ACCIDENT that my life and our house is full of Dominic's art.

> On Slate: "Night floods in at the bend of a knee"
> On Slate: "I wear the shadow of your bones like a tattoo"
> On Paper: "You come to touch my eyes"
> On Paper: "Inspired by the Song of Songs – July, 2000"
> On Paper: "J'aurais dû / y croire / mais entre la foi / et le regret / entre le corps / et la parole / sonnent les cadences / de l'exil"
> [I should have believed in it, but between faith and regret, between body and speech, ring cadences of exile]

I know these things by heart, par coeur, and I recite them to myself sometimes, in the car, on a walk, waiting in court ... both when I am enraptured by my husband and when I am deeply angry with him. These things fit with the best that we are and with what we can't always be. It's all incomprehensible except inside the colour orange, when he comes to touch my eyes.

Dominic, *Inspired by the Song of Songs*, from our wedding day, is indigo blue in the front hall, with the memory of your voice reading to us in the church. Indigo blue — colour of intuition and gnosis and healing. This is at the entrance to our home.

As for psalm 23, I did contemplate each line carefully on this day, as I was told to do. Only George would know me well enough to give me this task.

The Lord is my Shepherd. I don't like the idea of Lord, as in Lord and Master. I never have. I much prefer the United Church's softening and supplanting of the masculine God to the Anglican thees and thous. It's a struggle to think of the old man with the beard from the Sunday school colouring books ruling the world. Ted always referred to Yahweh, and I wish that I could let that roll easily off my tongue, but I can't. I wish it could just be about Light. I do think we are shepherded. I just can't think of the Shepherd as a "who." How about "The Light is my Shepherd?" That sounds like Star Wars. But I want it to be about Light.

I shall not want. But what about when it's really, really painful? I'm wanting. I want. This is mandatory, not permissive. Here's the lawyer in me. The fact that this is written *shall not want* instead of *may not want* means that this is a mandatory duty. Whose duty is it? Is it the duty of God, the gods, the universe, to create the conditions required to ensure that the duty is met — that I shall not want? Or is it a mandatory obligation upon me to not want. *I shall not want.* I shall accept. I shall have faith. I shall keep walking.

He maketh me to lie down in green pastures. This is about being led, haunted, and propelled. That's what this is about. But I still have a problem with the "He." Perhaps we are led, haunted, and propelled by a universal force that has been named the Holy Spirit, the Holy Ghost. An invisible bridge between the inner and outer worlds — between a quivering heart and the sound of the ocean. It may be simply a function of quantum mechanics. But, apart from all of that, I think that the only "he" who should maketh me to lie down in green pastures is my husband, which should be mandatory, as in "he shall maketh me to lie down in green pastures." That's why there should be a siesta in Canada. Canadians should take more afternoons off. Or at least I should.

He leadeth me beside the still waters. Stillness. Grace talked of stillness in her task to me — needing stillness to hear the message in the wind. Still waters are something else. Still waters require the absence of wind — at least no wind that can touch the water. I will need to think about that more. I am now fascinated by the idea of frozen music, like the Chladni plates and the Rosslyn Chapel. The Chladni plates, where a violin bow on a steel plate resulted in geometric patterns in sand, showed that a perfect resonance of the vibration of music and matter can be held in a solid and visible geometric form. In sand, through light, in water .... In us? Someone is working on developing a membrane that will freeze the Chladni vibrations of the whale song. It is about capturing an imprint — thinking of the water, and the wind, as a breathing web of immense rhythmic waves, and light and music as constantly resonating with matter. So when there is that perfect resonance, like what happened between my cedar flute and the voice of Patricia Elena in Panama, a child can say, "God is here." Stilling the water to find the frozen music.

He restoreth my soul. What is the soul? The soul is the thing we know but cannot touch. It is faith itself, the product of yearning for resonance, and when we feel it, we whisper to the Holy Spirit as it moves past and say, "God is here." There is no language for it. Humans just try to explain it the best they can. Whales sing it. But it has to be felt first, before it can be sung.

He leadeth me in the paths of righteousness for His name's sake. There are only two paths, two emotions: fear and love. It is a constant choice to be led toward love. Innocence is love. Maintain the stance of the wide-eyed innocent — and love. Don't fear.

Yea, though I walk through the valley of the shadow of death, I will fear no evil. This one, I get. I walk through the valley of the shadow of death. I know, George. I have always walked through the valley of the shadow of death. I fear death. Obviously. Palpably. Death is not something that has ever been hidden for me.

Before my mother died, while she was sick, I went to counselling with a Catholic nun at the hospital – Sister Aileen. I was not Catholic, but my mother used to be. I desperately wanted to know what was going to happen to my mother's body after she died. There was never a real answer for that. All they told me was that she would be buried in an air-tight, water-tight crypt where the water and bugs could not enter. How is that helpful?

After my mother died, I dreamt that she was buried in the front yard in front of the yellow lilies. In my dream, I dug her up with a tablespoon and no-one stopped me because they were too afraid. I also had a dream that she was in the operating room having her brain tumour removed and she died there. In the dream, I was in the hallway outside when the maintenance man came with a vacuum cleaner to suck her up.

I also fear evil. I see too much and always have. But believing oneself to be righteous and pure in the face of evil is, I think, more dangerous than evil itself. We are all the same, born of all the same possibilities, made of all the same stuff. It is foolish to believe otherwise.

For thou art with me; Thy rod and thy staff, they comfort me. I'm not sure about God. For thou art with me. Really? Can God see me? How is it that God can see me and everyone else at the same time? I think that is impossible. There are too many prayers to be answered, too much work to do. God probably burnt out and hit the brick wall a very long time ago. My walking poles are the only true comfort that I have had today.

Thou preparest a table before me in the presence of my mine enemies; thou anointest my head with oil; my cup runneth over. I don't like the idea of having enemies. If my cup runneth over, then what about the other people? Why would I get to sit at the table and not them? Why would I be anointed with oil? What about them? My enemy is fear. I will think of it this way: *The Universe prepareth a table before me in the presence of my fear, where by love my head is anointed with oil and my cup runneth over.* How's that?

Surely goodness and mercy shall follow me all the days of my life, and I will dwell in the House of the Lord forever. That would be nice – and it is a mandatory sentence, external to me. I'm just not sure if I believe it. Do you?

xoxox. I love you, too. J.

AT LUNCH, IN A SQUARE, I found a café full of old men, not pilgrims, and drank my café con leche happily among their banter and smoke. I spilled my water bottle under my chair and all the old men laughed at me.

As I left town I caught up to the "crazy Basque dudes" of blister fame and proudly matched my stride to theirs. We talked about the Basque witches. I told them that Proud Woman told me how to cook maple fish by layering maple leaves and fish on clay, sealing it, and placing it directly in the fire. The older man described a Basque tradition where sheep's milk is curdled into cheese by using leaves in the forest.

The conversation turned to witch burnings and torture in prisons, to false accusations and wrongful convictions, the determination of guilt and the meaning of justice. To trial by ordeal. In 1170, the King of Navarre believed his sister Sancia to be a witch. He arranged to have her tied hand and foot and thrown from a bridge into the river. Had she floated she would have been found guilty and carried ashore to be burned on the pyre but, innocent, she sank and so was saved by Lady Justice.

While talking, I also had the physical power to keep up. At the bottom of a long hill, everyone around me was slowing, but I pushed myself hard, striding past them all to the top of the hill.

Once there, panting and having left the others far behind, I was triumphant in my body and, finding myself on a hill, I turned to the wind and whispered Psalm 23. Dominic didn't say I had to shout it from a mountaintop. I whispered, but I whispered out loud.

And then carried on.

Love J.

9

I WOULD LIKE YOU TO PRAY on the rosary for the orphans in Russia.

Betty

Dear Betty:

TODAY WAS A REST DAY. After walking for nine solid days, this was the day that we were travelling to catch time. We only have thirty days and it takes longer than that to walk the full Camino Francés. Today I thought, as we sped along, that I will take a summer, perhaps next summer, and walk the full Camino Francés from St. Jean Pied de Port and then back on the Camino Norte, east across the coast, or the other way around. I want to follow the sun and my shadow in both directions, and that is what I think I will do. Someday soon.

Malakai and I had been planning to take the train, but we met some good Spanish friends who offered to drive us to Astorga. I have been walking with them for a few days and I was so very surprised to jump out of the Camino and into their Mercedes. It was odd to be in a car, covering the distance of the Meseta at high speed. I saw pilgrims walking and wondered what I was missing out there.

I woke this morning to three words in my mind. I was dreaming that I had received a text message from George with three words: "love, understanding, patience." I found this quite useful since Malakai has spent the last two days telling me that she does not want to walk with me anymore. She is being very difficult. Or she is finding me very difficult. Or perhaps both.

But, luckily, when the time came to jump into the Mercedes, she changed her mind and realized that I had indeed made some nice friends. Miguel and Oliva took us on a small detour to Yuso, where there is a monastery built with perfect proportions. The first written music is stored there, and we saw it, bound in leather and wood. The huge books contained the first Gregorian chants. It took my breath away. Frozen music.

We had a lovely lunch in the garden with the best Spanish ham and other treats. Oliva and Miguel were happy to be hosts to us, and we were spoiled with ice cream. In Astorga, we walked through the square and enjoyed the bells and cathedrals. Astorga is a city of sweets, and Miguel bought us cookies. We were told what to look for in Galacia, since they were leaving us here to go home. Boiled octopus is a delicacy and is called "pulpous coup coup." There is a Galician drink called quiemada that we need to find. On the way back to the albergue, I saw a decoration in a store window that was a carved house covered in witches on broomsticks. Because I had such a difficult time conveying the word "witch" to Oliva on the path two days before, I was so excited to find this display. I grabbed her and pointed, saying, "Look! Witch! Witch!" Malakai thought I was crazy, because she had not been there for the conversation.

Your task to me was left on my voicemail, and it's now vanished in the ether somewhere in Spain. I know that it was to pray Hail Marys and Our Fathers on the rosary for an orphanage in Russia, which I did, but not without some help.

My dear friend Felice brought me my last task the day before I left. The next day she returned with her mother's rosary. I wore the rosary on Day "F," I am wearing it today, and I will wear it into Santiago. Felice, knowing that I am not Catholic, printed out the Wikipedia lesson on the rosary and I fumbled through today as best I could. I hope that I did okay.

As I finish this letter to you, at the end of my journey, I have been thinking of something that was said one night at dinner by my new Camino friend, Suzanne, mother of Juli, both Canadians. I met Suzanne and Juli close to Santiago. Suzanne is about sixty and I love older women, having lost my mother, so I talked to her easily. I told her that I was doing these daily tasks, and she very perceptively asked me what I would do if I was not a lawyer. I have not decided to quit law, although at the start of my walk my thoughts did lead me to contemplate that as a possibility. Nearing the end, after firmly deciding that I do indeed love most of what I do in the practice of law, it was odd to be asked to contemplate other things that I might do instead.

As we talked more, Suzanne became convinced that I must write a book. My response to this was a vampire response, from all of the little vampires within that hold us back from doing anything brave. I said that my thoughts were not important or interesting to anyone but me. She strongly disagreed, so much so that I had to laugh and tell her that one of my tasks is to write the first chapter of a book in my head. That task is the direct result of my friend Jim reading the story that I wrote about you back in May.

Suzanne said that she does not like books that are written in the third person because she cannot insert herself easily into a third-person story. She said that even when she reads the Bible, she inserts "I" at every opportunity because it melds the gospel with her own experience. I found that very interesting, and as I sit here writing to you, I realize that the story that I wrote for you was in the first person, but referred to everyone else in the third person — you and Peter were "Mr. & Mrs. Ilkew," Kevin was simply "my brother." So I have decided now to rewrite it for you as it should have been written. And here it is, with love.

Dear Betty:

There are some things that I need to tell you.

When I was six years old, I always knew when it was Thursday. Or at least that is the day that I remember it being, the same time every week, when I would get up in the morning to have my toast and brown sugar and look out the kitchen window to see your sheets on the line across the low back fence.

The fences I remember in my childhood were different from the garrisons that separate houses in most places now. They were low, easy to jump across, easy to rest an elbow on, and easy to spray a hose over during neighbourhood water fights. Some adjacent yards, like ours and the Naimpallys', had no fences at all. That meant that the big butterflies that danced in the raspberry canes could be chased freely.

All of the yards had raspberry canes, and my dad's raspberries were bountiful. But they were not nearly as large as your raspberries, which poked through the back fence at places that became my favourite spot at certain times of the year. When the temptation became too great, I did hop the fence a least a couple of times to pick that big one just over there – and I have felt forever guilty for it. I'm sorry for stealing your raspberries.

Our gardens abutted each other, separated only by the fence. I remember dad digging exactly two rows per night, beginning in about April. The nightly work continued on through the summer, with the chatter and laughter over the back fence punctuated by your loud, life-filled laugh.

The sounds and sights grow distant, but are always there.

Kevin died after a quiet, decade-long struggle with autoimmune disease, kidney failure, a transplant, a parasitic infection, and failed life support. Two years before his death, I too developed an autoimmune disease that is, by all bets, genetically linked. We talked about it only once, and he told me that it was best not to dwell on these things. For himself, he simply carried on and rode his bicycle to dialysis three times a week, where he made some new friends, caught up on his sleep, and made the best of it. Kev had a gentle strength that he did not wear on his sleeve.

The night that Kevin received a kidney from an unknown stranger, Cathy and I slept in the white waiting room all night, draped over the metal arms of chairs that were bolted to the floor. Why bolt the chairs to the floor, I wondered? Was there concern that under the weight of worry and pain, furniture would be hurled from one end of the waiting room to the other? The most that happened to me that night was that somehow, in my tossing and turning, I bent the prong of my engagement ring and lost the diamond on the cold, white floor.

The next day, the transplant wing was full of new patients: Kevin and a second kidney patient, a heart patient, a liver patient, and a lung patient. The man who died must have been young and very healthy to be divided so fully among these people who now shared something so strange and foreign, deep within their bodies, touching their souls.

My brother had a fistula for many years to assist in kidney dialysis. An artery had been brought to the surface, where it was growing a smaller vein by force so that it would be able to withstand the dialysis needle. A good fistula becomes strong enough to fuel the dialysis machine three times a week for a very long time, if you are lucky.

Kevin's fistula was disgusting. It was, and looked like, a mass of artery and vein at the surface of the skin, bonded together in a sinewy ball that was just below his inner elbow. I couldn't look at it. I didn't want to be near it. He grabbed my hand and put it forcefully, but ever so gently, over the surface of the skin without making me touch it. His skin buzzed. His body sent vibrations through the fistula into the air above, and into my hand above that, with a power that was incomprehensible. It was a vibration so strong that I could hear the buzzing without there being a sound.

Then Kevin grabbed my head, in the way only a big brother can, and brought my ear down onto the fistula and held me there until my body relaxed. The buzz was gone, replaced by the rush of blood through the artery brought to the surface of the skin. The sound of life, normally so deep inside that I had never before thought that there could be a sound, was there in my brother's elbow. It was like an inner ocean. I stayed there, quiet and paying attention, for as long as he would let me.

I never asked to hear it again, although I longed to many times. And when he was dying, over the course of a month,

I was very far away from him and my irrational terror was that the sound would be gone and I would never hear it again. It was like when I gave birth to our last child, still-born at twenty-four weeks. The terror in that came from the knowledge that the birthing would be as it was, completely silent except for my own low moans.

When mom had her seizure when I was home alone with her, before I could even fathom what a brain tumour was, it was Peter who hopped the back fence and came running. I didn't see mom as she died, because they wouldn't let me. When she died, the family congregated – all of my sisters and Kevin, her sisters and brothers, and my father. On the first night, in the cold of January in Northern Ontario, you sent Peter and your boys across the back fence with enough food for an army. I can close my eyes and see them, out the kitchen window, coming over the fence like deer. You had company coming that night, which is why there was so much food available. I remember being told later that your company ate soup instead.

After Kevin's transplant, he recovered at my house for several weeks. I tried to make him as comfortable as I could, in the middle of my busy, overflowing house and life, but he needed to be well and be home, and there was a discomfort in that. But we managed and I am thankful for the time. Driving home one day, six deer crossed ahead of me on the road; I had never seen so many, so close. I came home to my kitchen and told Kevin about it. I like deer a lot now and I have many stories about them. I see so many more deer than I ever noticed before. They were probably always there, like the sound inside the fistula. I just wasn't paying attention.

At Kevin's funeral, I realized that he knew an awful lot of people for such a quiet guy. The other thing I realized is that it is very difficult to sob in front of strangers and then collect yourself to eat small pastries in the church hall, trying to remain upright and listen attentively to conversations that appear to be happening on another planet.

I looked up from such a conversation when I heard your familiar laugh and saw your smiling face, watching me from the edge of the crowd beside the coat-rack. I don't know if I have ever run to a person like that before, or if I ever will again, but on that day I leapt across the room to be folded into your arms with all of the sounds and smells of white sheets on the line, raspberries in the garden, real Jello popsicles, and hopping over the fences of my childhood.

Thank you.

Love J.

10

Task 1

Julie:

Alrighty, then, this is my decision, and it is final, no right of appeal of course, this is your Herculean task: Without any benefit of anything other than your brain, i.e, no maps, no looking up anything, as you are walking you are to name as many countries in the world as you can, keeping track of the number in your head, and here's how you score:

less than 80 = fail
80–100 = pass
100–120 = honours
120–135 = first class honours
greater than 135 = you can start calling yourself Jim!

Bon chance! Let me know how you do!

/JJ

Task 2

Julie:

I HAVE BEEN VERY REMISS. I hadn't read your dissertation. I just did. It is: truly beautiful. You have an enormous talent, you must not waste it any further writing pleadings and affidavits.

I have decided to change my trip challenge for you. Forget recitation of as many countries of the world as you can, how very mundane.

No, the challenge is this: Write the first chapter of your book, in your head if you like.

/JJ

RABANAL DEL CAMINO, JULY 11, 2009

Dear Jim:

I DID MY BEST WITH THE countries, but didn't come close to your record. On another day, I used your task as a diversion to stop a fight with Malakai and we named one-hundred-and-twenty-two countries, cooperatively, which I thought wasn't bad. It took two of us, though, one of whom is attending an international school with students from a hundred countries. Your score, therefore, is miraculous, and you remain the reigning champion. This is because, of course, you are a brilliant man.

As for the revised task, I think it will have to wait until the end. That's sort of the way this whole little "pilgrimage" thing is going.

When we last exchanged emails, I told you that I had to go and pack my platypus. I love my platypus, but I bought the largest size and that was a mistake. It is now being carried half full, or half empty – depending on your perspective. There are many *fuentes* along the way, so I can fill up as I go and thus carry a lighter load. I do miss the cold water resting on my back through my pack, but there are choices to be made on the Camino.

The platypus has been a constant in my daily routine. It is a bit of a finicky thing, with a long rubber tube that comes up through the top of my pack from which I can suck the water. If I'm not careful in the morning, the tube gets twisted and I have to rearrange absolutely everything to make the water flow, which is difficult. If I forget to close it off when I put my pack down, and the hose ends up underneath the pack, it causes a bit of a flood. It must be washed every night and hung to dry at bedtime to avoid bacteria growing inside.

On the first day in the Pyrenees, I was exhausted and put my pack down in the forest so I could sit. When I got going again and drank some water, my tongue and throat went numb. Obviously, I had not been careful about where the mouthpiece had landed, and it ended up on a toxic plant. I was terrified that I had poisoned myself, of course. I also couldn't drink any more water. It was a hard enough day as it was, never mind having to walk part of it with a numb tongue and no water. I have been much more careful since then.

The platypus is also a source of endless bickering between Malakai and me, because she has one too. I bought it in Toronto and brought it for her when I came to meet her. She was annoyed with me this morning and tossed her platypus across the floor while packing for yet another day, as in "Why do I need THIS?!... YOU carry it if you think it's so important!" There have been many of those conversations about who has to carry what.

Later in the morning, Malakai was walking far ahead of me when I came to a small church where a small woman was stamping the pilgrims' credentials. There was a witch water bottle with Dora the Explorer dressed as a witch, sitting on the window ledge of the church. I wish I had picked it up for Malakai to have instead of her platypus — not because of her mood this morning, but because today's theme was, yet again, witches.

There is nothing rational about this place. My conversations here revolve around witches, the intersection of religion and medieval life, the vibrations in the whale's song, the idea of the world as one of geometric shapes and frozen music, the meaning of light and sound and life.

I haven't had one conversation with anyone about child support or dividing up the snowmobiles and the children at the next court appearance. It is a blessed relief. I don't know how much more divvying up of "stuff" for people I can do in my life. It is not that I am unhappy about practising law — there are many things that I love about it. I just spend too much of my time doing it, that's all. And it limits me from being able, or being allowed, to think about the world in any other way. It is just amazing the things that human beings attach their pain to. From a distance, I can see that more clearly. I like walking. Walking doesn't involve the dividing up of anything. And I appear to be really good at it.

I also have to tell you that you were right about the part-time Master's degree in Law. The coursework is interesting, but I honestly could not care less about writing the papers, and I have successfully added yet one more weight on my shoulders. Completely true to form — you would think that I would have learned this by now! I thought that doing a Master's degree after finishing that year-long case in Toronto would lift me out of my dissatisfaction and lead me to think more broadly, about more things. I was also afraid of going blind, and I thought then that the LL.M. might give me the experience I would need to teach or do something else if I ever do go blind. You couldn't argue with that one, even when you were shooting down all of my other reasons. But I've changed my mind. As I walk, every time I think about the Master's degree, I think: "For what?!" and "Just because you can, doesn't mean you have to."

It's expensive, and unnecessary, and I should have listened to you. When I get home, I think I might quit, even though I have never quit anything before in my life. I think it would be good for me to actually quit something, don't you? Instead of writing the papers I need to write, I should just write something else. What do you think?

I had a fun time today chatting about saxophone music to a musician. His son plays French horn and his daughter plays the flute. Everyone in his town plays an instrument, he said. Why don't North Americans live like that? I have been working so hard for so long that I haven't played the piano in ages. I am trying to learn to play my cedar flute, but it's tricky. I need time to work on these things. I also need to learn how to swim because I don't know how.

I took swimming lessons when I was little. I clearly remember being a little "tadpole," and I was always slightly afraid of the water outside my own bathtub. I had the best little duckies who rode on yellow sponges in the bathtub, and that is where I was happy, every night. Almost every night in the summer, after my bath, my mom would put me into my baby-doll pajamas and my parents would take me to Dairy Queen to buy me a cherry Mr. Misty before bed.

The chlorinated pool was another story. When I was afraid to jump in, one of the swimming instructors picked me up and threw me into the pool. I was very, very small and so I was thrown far and deep. I have never been able to get over the feeling of not being able to breathe, deep under the water, so surprised at where I had found myself.

And at the lake, there were leeches. I hated leeches.

I have always loved the ocean, though. When I was twelve and my mother was sick, my sister and her husband took me and their children to Florida and I spent all my time in the ocean. I found a shell with a black pearl, and it was washed from my hands by the next wave. It was beautiful and I was sad to lose it. I wasn't afraid of the ocean, and I might have learned to swim well if it hadn't been so far away.

When we delivered Malakai to British Columbia last summer, we all took the train across the country and met Stefan in Vancouver before heading off to Tofino for a few days together. I really loved Tofino, and as we were walking in the town Malakai asked me why I hadn't moved to Tofino at age twenty-four to raise her as a hippy. It was a joke, but my response surprised me – it was that her dad had made the trip to Tofino when she was a baby, not me. And that was true. He did. I stayed put, hung onto my house, and raised my baby. Funny that she and I did the same trip, now that she is grown, without even realizing it.

We went out one afternoon to Meare's Island with a guide, the six of us in three sea kayaks. It rained the whole way. It was fabulous. George and I were completely out of sync when we started to paddle, and it was ridiculous, but once we caught our stride, we could have paddled to Hawaii, I'm sure. Meare's Island is the place where protests started in Clayoquot Sound, and it is a secret garden of ancient red cedar and small rivers. There is a two-thousand-year-old tree, with a hanging garden of amazing plants and creatures living on it. The realization that there is something that has been alive for two thousand years – not rock, not mountain, but a living thing – touched me beyond where I knew I could be touched. I decided then that I would become a sea goddess, to the complete dismay of my family.

But before I become a sea goddess, I must first learn to swim, so my intention is to sign up for lessons in the fall. I know that I can do this because in Mexico last March we sea-kayaked in a glass-bottomed boat so that I could see the fishes and coral, knowing that this was the only way I was going to see such things. I would not put my face underwater, especially with my eyes. What I did not know is that part of the excursion involved snorkelling. This resulted in the completely pathetic sight of me being towed by the guide with a little round life preserver, while the others in the group entered another world below. The guide was very patient and kind and decided, for some reason, to show me that I could do this too. So the next step was for me to put my face with the snorkel mask down through the hole of the life preserver, and be led around that way. My children were so embarrassed by me, but when my face was down and I stopped sputtering and caught my breath, I found myself completely alone in a green, blue, three-dimensional world that I did not know existed. Is our world on land as three-dimensional as this? Is the wind our water? Does our music carry?

The guide led me around on the life preserver and then dove to bring me up a starfish, which he placed right beneath my face. It was so beautiful and red, and he was so kind, that I found myself brave enough to let go of the life preserver, just a little bit, and swim on my own. When I came to the surface, I was triumphant and I saw the smiling face of my youngest daughter, Mary, who is eleven. I wanted to learn to swim right there, so that I could swim forever. There is nowhere to swim in Spain, but I keep talking to people about whales. I have to go and find some whales someday. Now that the Stefan boy is all grown up and settled on the East Coast, complete with his own sailboat, I bet he and I could find some whales. That would be a good plan.

As i think about this here, on the Camino, I am oddly happy that I have been such a ridiculous scaredycat about so many things. The feeling of triumph that I have now, at forty, is beyond measure. Breaking out of my own limits is like awakening to a new universe. I feel child-like. I am innocent. It is a beautiful, magical world.

Today, the path moved and meandered across the landscape such that I cast a shadow all day and was able to watch the rhythm of my feet and poles as I strode. Strode is the word for it – I strode into Rabajan del Camino where Malakai was waiting for me with her blue bandana, the ruckus over the platypus forgiven for today with an offering of yogurt, a peach, and a kiwi.

We stayed in an English albergue and I washed all our clothes with the smell of lavender in the air. I used the small clothes spinner, which was heaven on earth. Our clothes will definitely be dry by morning. This albergue has older people in it, and it is a relief to be away from the high energy and competition of the young pilgrims. Here, in this place, it is more cautious. There are "pilgrims' health" posters everywhere warning of various dangers, like blisters and strained tendons. There is no mention of tears and rage, which are the only dangers I have encountered so far.

Returning to your second task – did I write the first chapter of a book in my head? Maybe ... perhaps several.

I had many, many ideas – that's for sure. The mere thought of freeing myself to write was for me like unleashing an avalanche, so that was my day today: a steady stride and a steady stream of words and thoughts that had everything to do with my creative self, my whole self, and little to do with the lawyer self I left behind. This is a happier self, so I must say thank you. But you already knew that, smart man.

Maybe I'll write a whole book, and maybe I'll be brave enough to let you read the whole thing, since you are so encouraging of me in all things, in your very odd and unique way. But for now I'm just trying to write some letters that do justice to the beautiful, painful, difficult tasks that I have been given by my friends. That's it.

Love J.

11

OKAY, YOU ASKED FOR IT: I'd love you to recite, write, embody, meditate on, contemplate on, whatever ... every single quality about yourself that you LOVE. I want you to immerse yourself in a litany and catalogue of self-love. Enjoy.
Love, T.

Dear Tama:

I WOKE TODAY, DAY ELEVEN, IN the lovely English albergue to real strawberry jam and coffee. The garden was full of lavender, and the laundry tubs were full of clean water.

Malakai waited patiently for me and let me lead the way up the mountain this time. But at Foncebadon I became entranced with a circular Celtic house and she went on ahead, not realizing that I had stopped to look. I had a coffee, quietly, and heard about the history of this odd house – quite typical in Galicia with its original Celtic symbols intact.

I then met a Spanish Basque man and the conversation turned to persecution, traditional knowledge, and witches – my theme for the journey, it would appear. I had a virtually identical conversation with a French Basque man a few days ago. There has been much witchy talk.

We arrived at the pile of pilgrims' stones at the Cruz de Ferro after having shared a great many stories since Foncebadon. Malakai was waiting and angry, again, at having to wait for me. I was surprised that she had not gone ahead without me, as has been the recent pattern. Had I known that she would wait, perhaps I wouldn't have dawdled so much, but she is becoming frustrated with my pace and all of the distractions that seize me along the way. She has grown weary of me, and wants to be free. She did not want a stone for the pile. The man I had been walking with did not have a stone, so I gave it to him. I left my second stone from Proud Woman at the top.

I carried on with Malakai for a while and then she stopped in the road, angry, and said to me:

You did not include me in your stupid tasks, but my task for you is this:

Go on alone to Santiago
Be "nothing"
Have faith that I will be okay

She meant it. I had to take a deep breath, that's for sure. And I thought, "Great! On the day I'm supposed to write down what I love about myself, my child hates me and is leaving me. That'll be a good letter for Tama!"

But I let her go, with the promise that she would call or email George every night so we would know where she was and that she would be at the cathedral in Santiago at 7:00 every night until

I got there. I tried to change my mind and hers but she strode off. I made her wait long enough to tell her that I love her, which I do.

I waited on the road for a while, quietly saddened by the total failure of this journey. It was supposed to be about mother / daughter bonding and putting aside all of those adolescent things as she moves into adulthood, or at least that's what I had decided on the plane ride across the Atlantic. A failed mother and a failed pilgrim. What is to love?

But I couldn't stand forever, abandoned, in the middle of the road. I had to start walking, and as I rounded the corner I came to the entrance of an albergue covered in flags and other things. I went in because I was sore, my knee was hurting, and I saw that there was free coffee and a small shop.

There was an old man sitting on a bench behind where I was standing. Before I knew what was happening, he had led me to a bench and sat me down. My shoes and socks were taken off and I sat with my feet placed in the lap of the old man, without words and without language. There was no-one there who spoke English and no other pilgrims except me. It was only 10:00 a.m.

The old man began to massage and twist my feet such that at first I felt a tingling spread across my back and then I felt a vibration, or a shock, or something without words, run from the crown of my head to my tailbone and down to the ground. My spine started with the thing that it does, except so strong that I couldn't deny it or even be frightened by it, and I cried. The tears came with the relief of this knowledge that truly has no language. He took my hand and put it on my knee, where I felt warmth and tingling shoot into my hand and out my fingers. He squeezed my face, wiped my tears, and told me, I think, not to cry. And then he left.

I could do nothing but stay, and so I did. I was surrounded by grasshoppers. George had sent me a text message a few days before, when I said that I was not enjoying the endless fighting with Malakai and wanted to be alone. The text said, "You do not walk alone, grasshopper." Why is everybody calling me grasshopper? The same day he emailed Malakai to be patient because she might find that we needed each other. And yet here I was alone, surrounded by grasshoppers, rejected and abandoned by my daughter.

I had considered your task early in the day and felt it impossible. How can I itemize everything I love about myself when my child hates me? I told Malakai this morning that this was the task for the day and, as she was leaving me, she said something to the effect of "have fun with that!" That was before I entered Manjarin. For the remainder of this day, I gave no further thought to your task because there were so many other things going on.

After a couple of hours, an American mother and daughter arrived. The daughter is doing fieldwork for a Master's thesis about the Camino. Good for her. Not me. I decided yesterday to quit the part-time Master's degree in law. I am now a quitter, too.

They arrived just in time for lunch, and we were led inside to eat. The old man came back and sat across from me. As we talked, the young girl patiently translated our conversation.

The old man told me that he was only there at Manjarin for two more days — today and tomorrow — and that is why I am here today. He was waiting for me. He is a messenger for me and I for him. He touched my face and called me an angel.

He told me that the universe, and we in it, are energy and light, and that this is what I must know, and what he was waiting there to tell me. He went on to say that sometimes humans do not wish to return their light to the earth in human form because of human rules and constraints, and so they come as animals and spirit guides. This man writes poetry to the whales, asking them to share the ancient wisdom that they carry. He had a name for this but I can't remember what it was. He said all sorts of crazy things. If my spine hadn't still been moving and swaying and flooding through me, and if it were not a feeling that I knew as familiar from so many years of denying it, I would not have listened so intently and believed so much. But it was, and I had no choice. I also had no language to talk myself away from it. I could only listen to what was being said and translated in my direction.

After so much talk, I showed him the bear claw that I have been secretly carrying in my pack. Another man named Antonio, who had been watching and listening, became so excited that he took the claw from my hand and ran out the door. The young American girl said that he was excited because he had the thing that I needed and he was meant to give it to me.

Antonio brought my claw back with a piece of dark brown leather. He held it against a cedar pole and cut it on an angle with his knife, exactly as Glenn had told me it would need to be done. There is no magic in this, except that the movement of his hand down the pole was the same movement as Glenn's in the air before I left. It was amazing.

Does that not sound crazy? But there is too much happening to me for me to deny that it is happening. And it is not only in my head, because other people are always there and have witnessed all of these things, in pieces. When I put it together, it's overwhelming because this is not the path I am on. I am a lawyer. I have a real life.

You will remember when we were on the cruise in March that I was hesitant about many things. I stayed clear of Michael Beckwith, although he is fascinating, mesmerizing, even. The reaction of people to him was what made me uncomfortable — I found it slightly clawing and cultish and it freaked me out. But

I became friends with Linda from Hawaii and at one point she wanted a photograph taken of her doing reflexology on his feet. I laughed because there I was, on the lido deck, participating in this. Michael looked up, as I was taking the picture, having not spoken to me before. He started to tell a story, out of the blue, about being taken into a forest in Africa some years ago by a shaman. He looked at me and said, "You know, all of the ends of all of the branches of the trees lit up like a Christmas tree."

This was virtually identical to what Proud Woman had said to me in February. How can that be? It is becoming harder to talk myself away from the inexplicable power of whatever that is, and talk myself back into my regular life.

Antonio went away again with my claw, and came back with it properly strung, with a small bell. He tied it and put it around my neck and I kissed him, without hesitation, on both cheeks. I was so grateful. I have never been given such a gift, and he knew it. A few minutes later he came and took it from my neck again, and this time returned it with a white feather.

The old man told me that Finisterre is the true finishing point of the Camino, where the sky and the sun and the water meet. He told me that Finisterre is a place of magic and that I must end there. I don't know what to believe of all of that. I just know what I believe in the marrow of my spine.

You realize, of course, knowing the things that you know, that I could not have planned this in a million years, so it must be real. I can hear you laughing as you read this and I am so glad to be writing to you on this day. You will not think I am crazy, so I can tell you all of it without reservation. Imagine two lawyers having a conversation like this! How many law degrees does it take to change a light bulb? Or find the meaning of life?

As for your task, I have loved my child in letting her go today, and I have loved myself in allowing myself to stay. What do I love about myself? Everything on this journey so far is about realizing that I am both everything and nothing. Oddly, that is what Malakai said to me as she left. "Walk the rest of the way alone and be nothing! You are nothing!"

"You do not walk alone, grasshopper," says my beloved husband from afar.

Sitting under the flags all afternoon, writing and listening to the wind as Grace has told me, high in the mountains, surrounded by butterflies and grasshoppers, I was happy. In this crazy place, full of crazy people, I was calm. My spine was flooding and pulsing and I wasn't afraid. I was very, very happy and felt very, very blessed. Truly.

As I walked up the last hill before getting to this place, and before being left by Malakai, I had been thinking about my sisters. I love my sisters and I decided that my dad is right – life is simply about putting one foot in front of the other until you walk off the cliff. Life was in Kevin's fistula and it is in my steps. That's it. I want to tell my sisters that. I want them to know that. Paso por paso. Step by step. We are all so afraid.

Toward the end of the afternoon, five friends travelling together from the Czech Republic walked in from Astorga and decided to stay. There was also an Italian man who slipped in, alone.

Before dinner, I went to the edge of the field with my flute and tried to play my notes, alone, surrounded by the grasshoppers and the wind. It is hard to play my flute in the wind. For one of my tasks, I have been trying to learn a new note each day while being quiet inside an imaginary soft space. I have found this hard to do each day, because to be inside my imaginary little sky-blue egg, I need to be alone. I have to either find a place to sit while walking, or wander away from the albergue in the evening. Sometimes

I have had to imagine my egg while in the bathroom behind a closed door. Sometimes I have my flute and play, but other times I've been too embarrassed to pull it out, and I just have the memory of the one note that I am good at in my mind. This morning I played my note at the mound of pilgrims' stones, to show the Spanish Basque man, and Malakai was mortified. I think perhaps that is why she has left me.

While I was playing, one of the Czech boys came and sat quietly behind me, listening. I didn't know he was there. People keep sneaking up on me like that. We sat on the hill for a while and then made our way back for dinner. It was a lovely dinner, although there was very little common language. I think that perhaps in the middle of all of the events of this day, I have eaten octopus without realizing it. At dinner, we discovered that Manjarin is a Templar community of nine, with five year-round residents in this albergue. Antonio took the Italian and me to see his many dogs, which are half wolf, "lobo." He also raises chickens. We were told that the Templars have always and forever held this place for pilgrims.

At dusk, the old man again returned and this time fixed on the Italian. I watched and he took his hands and talked to him at length. I watched the Italian's face move from shock to wonder to gratitude. I couldn't understand what was said but I understood his face as I watched. While I was watching, Antonio took my right hand between both of his hands and I felt a river flow through my palm to my shoulder, so much so that after he let me go I spread my fingers wide and felt as though flames would shoot from them.

During all of it, the Italian and I were watching each other, without language. He and I have each experienced something extraordinary today, although the details are yet unknown. I was so happy to have a friend in this — it was comforting to have it understood by someone else, even if we couldn't speak. It was also good to have a witness so that I can assure myself that I have remained sane. This day really happened.

It really did.

We are preparing for sleep and I must return to your task. I am having a hard time cataloguing myself. I can do nothing but lie on my stomach — feeling large and luminous. My spine has not stopped all day and I am not afraid, as I feel it rock toward the sky. I have had a hard time finding any words at all to describe this day. There are no words. There is only this.

And so I am going to return to something George said right before I left, which was for me to remember that he loves me for being the pure spirit of light that I am. He said it with a George grin and it was a light and frivolous thing to say, said in the way that only my husband can say such a thing. But tonight as I am lying here, I feel love all around me and I love myself for being the pure spirit of light that I am. I do. I am. That is all that I am. That is the lesson of this day.

Love J.

12

Hi Julie. Here goes.

GRATITUDE JOURNAL OR GRATITUDE PRAYER

At the end of the day, list five things you are most grateful for, e.g.. shoes, Spain, ice-cream, Kleenex, God or whatever. Have a great trip.

God Bless. Fran.

PONFERRADA, JULY 13, 2009

Dear Fran:

I WOKE UP AFTER THE MOST wonderful day yesterday and I was full of gratitude, full to the brim, and so it is perfect that I have arrived at your task today.

Last night at 10:00, as we were rustling ourselves into bed in the attic room of the medieval albergue at Manjarin, the music started: "Jesu, Joy of Man's Desiring." Malakai had gone on ahead and I was alone.

There was a Czech group of two men and three women who began to sing a lullaby. Another man, an Italian, and I were each lost in our thoughts of the day. Before the singing started, we were both scribbling madly in our journals. After that, we were simply sung to sleep. I have not had anyone sing me to sleep in a very long time. The lullaby was called "Between the Mountains" — in Czech, of course.

When I woke this morning, it was again "Jesu, Joy of Man's Desiring." That was the song that led me down the aisle, between Stefan and my father, when George and I finally got around to getting married.

That was a fun wedding, with my perfect silk shoes moving past the string quartet in the afternoon, only to be destroyed by square dancing in the rain into the wee hours. At the church, we had beautiful music and beautiful readers: Brian reading the prayers, Kiki and Malakai reading from Romans, Stefan from Matthew, and Dominic from the Song of Songs. At home, our house and our life were full. A perfect day. And "Jesu, Joy of Man's Desiring" makes me remember all of it.

We also woke this morning to a large bell being rung and the dogs outside beginning to howl — to our great amusement. These dogs are apparently half-wolf, a multi-generational family of mixed species, cared for by a man named Antonio who loves them. George says that dogs have no "inner dog" — they simply are. Humans are too afraid to be. It's not the same for us.

Downstairs, breakfast was on the table — biscuits, jam, juice, and coffee cooked on the stove with hot milk. All of us lingered, not wanting to leave this place, quietly taking turns at the squat toilet, and returning to the kitchen, shuffling about in slow preparation for departure.

Others began to arrive, pilgrims off to an early start. They entered not knowing what we had experienced in this place the previous day, and I felt then that this was the mix on the Camino — there are those who pass through certain places, and others who must stay. The place is not always the same, nor are the people. Here, there are those who stop for coffee, browse the makeshift outdoor shop, and carry on – and then there is me, who arrived at 10:00 yesterday morning and couldn't leave.

This place, this walk, is like Agda's egg, from my task on the third day. The container is the only thing that must stay the same. The colours, the music, and the people who carry these things simply flow through.

It is hard to describe what happened at Manjarin. I tried yesterday in my letter to Tama. And I must try again today in my letter to you, but I think I will fail.

There was an old man who spoke only Spanish and showed me, without language, the meaning of faith. He did this by rubbing my feet and allowing something to pass into me. He opened me up and gave me proof of something that I did not know I was searching for. The old man described the place where we were at Manjarin as an energy site. In Australia, indigenous peoples have travelled and sung along "songlines" – the paths were themselves experienced as music. Perhaps this is true of the Camino too.

I thought today that this is what they mean by the grace of the Holy Spirit. It is energy and it is light and it moves through matter, through us, into everything. Some cultures think that a child is born with a song, deep in its being. Today I decided that perhaps it is that song of our birth that seeks resonance and tries to find God. The Holy Spirit is one name for the larger energy of the universe, and it has a song too. It is about resonance. That's it. I felt it deep in my core.

While we were preparing to leave, the old man came back and the Italian and I were both obviously overjoyed to see him again to say thank you, after having had a night to contemplate the gifts he had given. We both hugged him, and he put one hand on each of our backs. Some of the others came close. It was a very powerful thing that was happening, and I felt wrapped by a circle that spiralled to the centre of the earth. It is impossible to find words to describe it. Shortly after that, I put on my pack and was the first to leave that magical place.

One of the last things that the old man said to me, through one of the Czech girls who could just barely translate, was not to worry for my *chica* but to keep my eyes open because she would be sitting and waiting for me in a town along the way. This was because Malakai left me yesterday and I did not know where she was.

As I left, a man named Antonio, who had helped me finish a beautiful necklace the day before, rang a bell long and hard for me until I was out of sight.

I spent the morning without water because there was no running water at Manjarin. I went up and down the Cordillera without pain in my knee and without feeling the weight on my back. I came to the first town and stopped for coffee, the time of those first five kilometres having passed so quickly. I was amazed at the progress of my strong body. The next five kilometres were similarly effortless, the only effort now being in my thoughts. My feet are used to this now. My mind, on the other hand, is reeling.

I thought of all of the coincidences and all of the goodness in this life and I was, indeed, grateful for this day, for my freedom on the mountain, and for having such friends, both at home and now here, in this place.

I was not worried about Malakai. In fact, I was very, very proud of her, and I thought a great deal about her birth, her childhood, mistakes that I have made, and things that we have had to endure, and I hoped truly that she would not stay angry with me for my very real flaws as she moves into adulthood and I become the mother of an adult woman.

I will be the mother of three adult women, in the end.

In about three villages, I think, I was considering stopping to eat but wanted to carry on in the hope of catching up to her in Ponferrada. As I was passing one of the last cafés in the town, I heard a small voice off to my left: "Mommy...." Malakai was indeed sitting and waiting. She'd had a difficult time without me the day before because of the circumstances of her day, which somehow involved having to go five kilometres back up the mountain. I suggested that there was a lesson in this for her that she would return to later in life. And I was grateful to her for abandoning me, because I would not have stopped and stayed in Manjarin otherwise.

It would appear, however, that Malakai and I are once again travelling together. Ponferrada is a large town, so I decided to check us into a hotel and go for some ice cream near the castle where we could pretend to be fairy princesses. We also went to the post office, which at long last was open! We are half-way to Santiago in terms of our days of travel, and my pack is now familiar and quite light. Despite this, I decided to ship 2.7 kilos on to Santiago. I really don't need to carry two pairs of sunglasses, a chafing stick, and foot-odour spray. These are not essential.

This is the first time in my life that I have ever given any consideration to what something weighs. Even my "platypus," which is used to carry my water, is filled only half-full now because there are plenty of places to fill up and no need to carry more. I know now that I can carry everything in my pack, but that doesn't mean I have to. So today, at the post office, I filled a small box and sent it away.

I can't wait until the lightness of tomorrow. I will run through the mountains. I will dance with the butterflies. I will jump with the grasshoppers. I am grateful for lightness and for laughter.

I have missed both. My days on the Camino have been reduced to such basic routines, and yet I feel that I am living in an ever-expanding universe.

I am, indeed, grateful. I have written each day about what I am grateful for, and here is my full list:

finding Malakai
Marty Murphy
the wizened priest at the pilgrims' mass
the man who told me where to put my shoes
cow bells
the shower
the yellow foam mattress
butterflies
the company of Undewe
time walking alone
the bathroom
the city
no blisters
my walking poles
the music
water
breath
sleep
sky
wind
snails
sight
freedom
solitude
stones

new friends
arms
sand art
chocolate
Malakai's blue bandana
thistles
sunflowers
wheat
strength
muscles
endurance
stamina
rhythm
laughter
language
hands
bells
windmills
the rosary
light
ham
ice cream
chanting
my flute
my platypus
wisdom
words
thoughts
starfish
oceans
translation

thong

owl feather

paella

coffee on the stovetop

Jesu, Joy of Man's Desiring

grasshoppers

wind chimes

toilet paper

castles

sundaes

my child

clothespins

massage

my dog

cherries

isolation

George

a long day walking

sleep

courage

mountain tops

butterflies

challenges

triumphs

imagination

history

soil

shoes

socks

raspberries

cheese

soap

peaches

glass

my towel

sunglasses

Mary Anne

Barbara

Agda

Ted

Elvira

Felice

Grace

Dominic

Betty

Jim

Tama

Fran

Meredith

Brian

Lisa

Peg

Glenn

Ross

Sylvia

Janette

Suzan

Evelyn

Joe

Murielle

Sue

Nancy

Garth
Malakai, Stefan, Kiki, Mary
mom & dad
Mr. Mistys and baby doll pajamas

Love J.

13

IT DIDN'T TAKE ME BUT two seconds to figure out a task for you to complete while you are away. I think this will combine a bit of everything — emotional, physical, and spiritual.

Using the last few episodes as a base, examine how and why (even with the bitter sting of prior experience) you repeatedly fail to identify those who will end up hurting you, instead inviting them wholesale into your life. Reflect on the parts of your own personality and emotional state that crave the repetition of this scenario. What is it you need from these situations that hasn't yet been satisfied?

I look forward to hearing about your other tasks — if you are sharing!

Hugs.

M.

Dear Meredith:

THANKS FOR THE TASK, MEREDITH. Really. This is something that, in my life, only you could say. And then follow with "Hugs"!

The answer is yes, I am an idiot. And yes, I am a bad friend to those who truly care about me. I know that. The question you are asking is why....

I thought of this all day, truly, and I don't know if I have an answer. It came up over and over again as Malakai and I walked, which we did together for most of the day today. That is a first. We have been at cross-purposes, she and I. Today I worked very, very hard to listen to her about all sorts of things. You know more about mothers and daughters than I do, since you still have a live mother and have moved through all the stages that I missed altogether.

Part of listening hard, both to Malakai and to my task from you, involved fighting my demons and defences and holding my tongue. In doing this, I also came to several parts of an answer to your question.

I have never ever believed that I have a limit. In my mind, there is no limit to what I can accomplish, to what I can absorb, or to what I will accept.

I have not, in forty years, said "no" to very many things. I have, according to Malakai, hidden this fact behind a series of decisions that have meant "I have to" — not for myself or for my family, but for reasons that I can't explain. That is the real question, isn't it?

In grade two, there was a poster on the classroom door with a chart for everyone's name and the days of the month. For each day, if you did something really good, you got a gold star. If you did something very bad, you got a black mark. I was smart and I was good, and I never got black marks. Except one day, when the teacher put someone else's black marks in my space and I was distraught. I can still feel that feeling in the pit of my stomach. Even when the teacher put three gold stars on top of the black marks to cover them, I still knew they were there.

I was always praised as a small child, and as a result I fear judgment almost as much as I fear death. I don't want anyone to put a black mark in my space. The people stuff has always mattered to me. People are important to me. And I am not very careful.

I don't want to be a selfish girl; I want to be praised, so I don't say no. And I have not valued myself or my true and dear friends enough to protect my privacy and my time. I want gold stars from everybody, even if they are complete jerks. This has led me to accommodate myself in ways that are truly ridiculous. Especially when I read this, in black and white in front of me, and I know that it is true. I have not honoured very much about myself and the beauty that is my life.

Part of it is a girl thing. Part of it is a me thing. Part of it is a gold star thing. I sit with feelings for years, preferring the easy way, the nice way, preferring not to be alone to figure it out. The fact is that I let it all in, I absorb it all, take it all, mold it all, give what I can which is never enough — and then say "no" in all the wrong places, with my family or children, or with the right people when it's far too late. It is very confusing for all involved. I think that is what I do. I worry way, way too much about all of the ridiculous people stuff that gets in my way.

Yet, when I did my A-Z list, I picked the names and sent the emails with almost no thought. Some of the emails to old, old friends started with "I know I've been a bad friend, but...." Still, it's interesting that I absolutely knew who to ask, and it's a bit of magic and good luck for me that, after being first and always a lawyer for almost a decade, I still have at least twenty-six people who care enough about me to set my tasks and make me take stock. I don't think that very many intended that directly, except of course you! Yet this is the cumulative effect of the last thirteen days, with fourteen more to go.

I did not ask for a task from anyone who might think themselves entitled to pronounce upon my life "in that way." You know what I mean. I knew this exactly. The truth is that I should listen to my gut more – if I did, perhaps I would not endlessly be reflecting on the bitter sting of past experience. I always, always know the difference between what is real and what is pretend. I just ignore myself and let the vampires in.

The other interesting thing is that I did not ask George or the kids for a task. In every family there is a measure of pain and trauma, and we, as you well know, are no different. I intended a walk that would be quite free of all of that and thought that by keeping my mind busy with tasks, I could merrily skip along down the Camino with my busy brain kept busy.

I know that circumstantial and superficial relationships, based largely on proximity and some sort of mutual need, have not served to propel me forward. I have monopolized my time in this way, in my office world, and I've been a bit stuck for the eight years that I've practised law. I have practiced with significant success, but not without removing me almost completely from, as Malakai says, "normal" people. I have sat in restaurants and airports and other public spaces and have listened with interest to how lawyers talk to, and about, "normal" people. I have never thought that this is what I've become or am in danger of becoming, but I think the danger is there. Perhaps this is not something peculiar to lawyers – it may be endemic to everyone whose identity and self-worth become entirely connected to their work. It's a slow, invasive progression. This happens mostly to professionals, I think, because the professional culture and the pressure of work creates self-perpetuating justification as an occupational hazard.

And so I have been surrounded by other professionals, and by staff, and by people who are generally doing things during the working day in close proximity to me. Energy poured into some of these relationships has been completely and totally consistent with the rest of the stickiness of my life.

I decided on a mountain a few days back that my life has been far too sticky. "Quick! Hug the tar baby! It will be different this time – you'll see!" Am I right, dear Meredith?

Considering this, and reflecting on the task at hand, I asked myself what I have been hiding from in my work. I think you know the answers to that as well as I do. Perhaps you know more. I am hiding from all of the things that I've been thinking about here, for two weeks solid.

Law school was an escape for me – you know that. Work has been much easier than real life, and in a lot of ways I'm better at it. I have used it as a bit of a cave – I have retreated from all of those other parts of my life that were slightly messy and not nearly as ordered as case law and precedent and the Rules of Civil Procedure.

AND SO, MEREDITH, I HAVE been lazy and inattentive and afraid. I don't want to be where I'll hear what I don't want to hear. I know that. So do you. "Excuse me, Julie…," says Meredith. "Where are you?" I know. I know. I've been running. I know. Malakai asked me what I was before I became a lawyer. That was a tough one. I told her to talk to you. (Just be careful what you tell her.)

Remind me that I have to play you a song on Oliver Schroer's *Camino* album — of feet walking on the Camino. The way it is recorded means that when you are wearing earphones, the feet walk right through your head. It makes me laugh every time. Perception — it is all about whose version of perception we are working with, isn't it?

I think that before I was a lawyer, I might have been a better friend, a better spouse, a better mother. That is almost enough of a sad realization to make me decide to quit forever. But now that I have no staff, I don't have to work as hard to keep the machine running. It's a choice and one I should have made a long, long time ago. I've also decided to quit the stupid Master's degree. Was it you or Kevin who said, "Don't you already have a Masters degree?" Yeah, okay. I quit. Can you believe it? I'm going to quit something! We should have a party.

So, finally, in answer to your question — I really don't know why it's so hard for me to say no to the bullshit. It's hard for me to write anything about this at all, and that is pathetic. In my Maslow's pyramid of needs, I am stuck in the bottom layer of bullshit. I just don't know. Maybe it'll come to me down the way a bit.

As soon as I get back and get my head straight, I'll come for a visit and we'll find a place to have some yummy martinis. I'm glad you are still there....

Love J.

14

WHAT ARE MY FORTY YEAR old fears? If I did not hold these fears, what would I be doing?
Brian

LA FABA, JULY 15, 2009

Dear Brian:

WELL, I SUPPOSE I WOULD be doing this. This is a start.

Oh, Brian, it is so, so hard. Today I am past the half-way point and I'm tired. I had thought that I was beyond the painful, painful days, but I now realize that I am walking in waves. Yesterday, I was at such a loss to answer my task from Meredith because I was so sad for wasted energy and wasted time and the fact that I have been ignoring – hiding from – some very dear friends.

And today, you have essentially asked me to consider that the last forty years of my life have been ruled by fear. Ouch. That is not how I read the task initially when you gave it to me. But this morning as I read it, on day fourteen, it felt that way. Because, if I am honest, I have already had fourteen days to think about exactly that, and I am full of sorrow and regret.

But climbing to the top of another mountain today, something huge shook loose. I was thinking about all of the thoughts of the last days and the odd mix of fear and driven energy that is my life. Are they forty-year-old fears? Maybe. Thirty years of fear, for sure. Today you have made me turn to face both my ten-year-old self and my daughter – and it was so awful.

When my mother died, I was obviously there but easy to overlook in the busyness of it all. My brother stuck with me. It was Kevin who took me to the casket to see her after the funeral director had thrown the bifold doors open and I was not prepared for what I saw.

I remember the sound of those doors running along the rails, and I remember my mother's face in the distance under a light. When we were at the casket, I couldn't look at anything but her pinky finger and I whispered to Kevin that it moved. He held me and hugged me and was the perfect big brother. I always loved him.

A few months after my mother died, I packed up her clothes and things, alone in her bedroom with her lingering smells. I did this because my dad wanted to move back into the bedroom. My sisters didn't come to help me. It was not my brother's job. I wrote a list of the contents of each box on the lid with a magic marker, in my childish bubble handwriting. Wigs, pantyhose, kerchiefs, button box.

When Kevin died, I couldn't bear it – but I also had to tell my dad that he was dead and so had to pull myself together and be a big girl. I went to Centennial Place to tell him, and he cried just a little. I couldn't hold it together and ended up spread across his lap like a small child. He rubbed my head and told me that I had always had a hard row to hoe. That was a missing piece after my mother died. No-one held me while I cried, except for my brother

— and he only did that beside my mother's casket. And now he's dead.

THE DAY MY BROTHER DIED, my dad told me a long story of his most painful regret, a story that I had never heard. Kevin had been a very good baseball player, but he was gentle and the other boys could be rough with him. He was a good pitcher, and my dad gave him the advice one day that he should pound the ball at a particular kid who had been tormenting him. It is probably something that my father's father would have said to him, because my dad was a very gentle boy too. Kevin did what my father told him and hurt the other child. My dad told me that Kevin was angry with him and told him that he was wrong. My dad said that this was true — that Kevin had never hurt anyone and didn't ever want to. He had never apologized to Kevin for it. And now he's dead. I spent a lot of time today thinking about the things we try to put words to and why. And the words we hang onto until it's too late.

There is a letter that my mother wrote me when she was sick. She wanted me to be a good girl and a big girl, and to be strong. In a fragile state one night a couple of years ago, after almost losing my eye again, I found myself alone in my car, driving and screaming "I'm not a big girl!" out loud, out the window, on an empty country road.

Today I walked through these thoughts and saw my mother's hands in the casket, her pinky finger tucked beneath the small white flowers placed in her hands. I happen to be wearing the pinky fingernail of a bear around my neck, which is a whole other story that I will explain later when I am home. How many mountains does the Camino have to cry on, I wonder? This particular part of the Camino is said to wind through mountains that are like the fingertips of the world. As I came to the top, I thought of myself standing on the pinky finger of the mountains that surrounded me, and the words came, out loud: "Mommy, can you see me?"

Am I a big enough girl? A good enough girl? Have I done okay? I can't believe I said it out loud, but I flooded that mountaintop with tears I didn't know I had.

Then, when I finally got moving again, I rounded the corner with my puffy red eyes behind my sunglasses to find Malakai sitting in the dirt, waiting for me. She handed me a letter and told me that she didn't want to talk to me again until I had read her letter. She walked away and I was alone, waiting for my mother to see me, watching my daughter leave. I have never felt so alone and so bare. I did not want to read her letter. I knew what it was going to say. "Mommy, can you see me?"

I stood at the edge of the path, splayed on the edge of the hill, and I sobbed from the pit of my being. I could not catch my breath. It was so much worse than the fourth day, which has been my worst day so far. On the fourth day I couldn't breathe either and had walked with a mantra that was given to me in my task for that day: Guide / My / Feet / Love.

Today was the bookend to what started then – I know that, and I will have to show you. On this day, my forty-year-old fears cracked open and there was a flood. That's what happened to me. It was desperately physical and frightening and I had to keep changing mantras to be able to breathe. I worked my way through a pile of them. God knows how long I was up there:

Walk / Through / The / Pain
Listen / To / The / Wind
I / Shall / Not / Want

You / Are / An / Angel
Right / Left / Right / Left
Can / You / See / Me

Only the first and the last of these words were mine. All of the other words were gifts that I have been given and have picked up along the way here. I realized this today, and they helped me so much. Just words, but all of them — all of them — carried love to me when I truly needed it. I was so alone up there.

If people don't have these things and each other to rest on, perhaps that is when they become unhinged. Or cruel and hateful. Or arrogant and disconnected. I am so lucky.

When I was finally calm, I sat and read Malakai's letter. There was nothing written that I didn't know. Eventually, I picked myself up and caught up to her much farther down the way. After the rest of the long day of walking, and talking, and justifying, and backtracking with my child, I am surprised at how much I have given her to carry without meaning to, and how much of my own fear I have passed to her. She wanted me to understand her emotions as they had been in her early adolescence, emotions that she felt, and held, during a time when I was preoccupied with all of the other things, the other crises. To her, all of the crises seemed to, and in fact did, follow one upon the next. You, of course, know all of this. I'm not sure how any of us are still standing.

Through the rest of the day I tried very hard to listen, but it was so difficult to hear it, and I felt all of the reflexes kick in — sadness to anger, fear to pain — push it out, push it away. I was angry with her for making me see things I already knew, and for saying it out loud. But I couldn't stay angry — we were on a path in the middle of nowhere, so there was nowhere to hide. I couldn't hide from myself. I couldn't hide from her. We will get through it, but I have decided at the end of this day that I am walking in the middle of hell on Earth.

What would I be doing if I didn't have my forty-year-old fears? I'm changing my answer. I would not be here.

Instead of this endless painful walking in this foreign place full of tears, I would be the two-year-old child in the home movies dancing in the living room in pure delight – loving the world with my whole heart and having it love me back. I would love myself for being the pure spirit of light that I am. And I would love my life for reflecting the pure spirit of light that it does. Right now. No matter what.

That's what I would be doing. Can I do that?

Love J.

15

THIS WAS EASIER THAN I thought ... I believe you get Tama's monthly mailing but if not, this is a passage from the last one (it has stuck with me since I read it).

> Years ago, I witnessed the perfect metaphor for this secret self. I live in Colorado where it tends to be sunny and dry. One year we got more moisture than usual. Later that week, I had new plants present themselves in my garden. They just sprung up. Of course when I saw these new flowers that I'd never planted, I wondered if I had been blessed by the handiwork of urban fairies. But a gardener friend had another explanation. She told me that the seeds had always been there. Until now, they hadn't gotten sufficient moisture. But with the new weather conditions, the seeds had finally gotten what they needed to grow into their potential.

Your "O" task, grasshopper — should you choose to accept it — is discover the hidden seed inside of you that is going to thrive (perhaps it's already started by the time you get to "O") now that you've given the seed a whole new set of conditions to grow in by experiencing the Camino Trail and the wonderful expedition you are on.

Lisa

Dear Lisa:

TODAY WAS A LONG DAY, fuelled by the exhaustion of a larger Mother / Daughter (Capital "M"; Capital "D") Day yesterday. Malakai and I both had to quietly drag ourselves up and down twenty-five kilometres worth of Galician mountains. I got my first blister, and it rained on us for the last hour (a first).

A seed? What will grow? I have a good analogy for that, from a horrid portion of the Camino way, way back. It was another hard day – the fifth – and I was walking along a very dirty, dusty, clay-baked part of the path. I could only think of how ugly it was and how nothing could grow in the clay. Like half of my front yard where the trees and bushes on one side are so stunted and there is nothing I can do. It's just the fact of trying to put roots down in the stupid clay. My thoughts on the fifth day were pretty much this: "Enough! I quit! Do you hear me?" Stupid, awful, clay path.

I passed a creepy cemetery that day and didn't want to look in. I found myself looking down to the right and I saw the very tip of a snail shell poking out of the clay. I dug it out. And then another. And then another. I sat in the clay and made a small pile of snail shells. I have been carrying them ever since.

Where on earth did the snail shells come from? I never imagined shells as big as that on land. A few days later I found the answer. The snails cling to thick blades of grass by the hundreds, and when they die they fall to the ground and are buried. I have a beautiful picture, which I will show you. It is exactly what you are talking about. There is a magical geometry to these shells – I have spent a lot of time pondering them on the path since I am now carrying all of them with me. Snails are also very sensual beings, according to people who have seen them up close.

The spiral of the snail shell apparently follows the Fibonacci series of the golden section. They say that geometry and mathematical ratios, harmonics, and proportions are repeated throughout all of creation: in nature, in music, in light, in cosmology. I walked though a spiral path way, way back. The spiral was made of green growth. It was amazing. I'll have to show you the picture. Seeds are the same. The arrangement of leaves on a stem is the same. The holding of the perfect imprint of a symmetrical flower in the small seed is a daily miracle that we could try to understand but don't. Most of the time, it's hard to even notice at all. In my life, at least, I am so preoccupied with the human drama and human tragedy that the physical world often doesn't exist – even though it is right in front of me.

People will tell you that on the Camino there is a magical hexagonal church in the middle of nowhere, at Eunate. I heard about it but didn't visit. They say that geophysicists and hydrologists have found inexplicable convergences of water and energy in the undercurrents of that place. I wonder if it's like the Rosslyn Chapel in England, where symbols in the stone are apparently organized in harmonic and melodic progression. That would be an amazing thing, if it's true.

These are definitely things that I have to ask my friend Garth about, because he understands math. Everything about me and my life is verbal. I only did well in one math subject – calculus – because it used letters instead of numbers. I don't understand any of the rest. There is no distance, or space, or measurement, or vision that I have ever been able to hold and understand. Is that a left brain / right brain thing? Are girls just not good at math? I don't think that's true. I think I should become good at math so that I can answer my own questions.

I have many competing thoughts, here on this Camino, of how I should spend my time and my health. I will keep practising law – that much I have decided. But I am going to have to be very, very careful with it.

I will also become a sea goddess, but first I have to learn to swim. I will become a math genius, like Garth. I will learn physics. I will be in my garden. I will learn to feed myself. I will stay strong so that I can walk this Camino at age seventy, like the woman from Belgium who travelled 2,200 kilometres from her front door to Santiago, and camped alone for much of the way. I will become the consummate polymath – a Renaissance chick. That's what I will do. I have as many seeds in me as there are days in the rest of my life.

To do this, I need to spend some time away from all of the people stuff and live in the physical world. I need to get out of one hemisphere of my brain and into another. I need to get on with it, and forget about what all of the other people think / need / want. That is where I will try to start. I have to stop being pulled in all directions by all of the people. I want to move beyond all of that.

Except for my husband, of course. And my children. And my friends. But I am going to be very, very careful with all of that too.

I can't start today, though, because today I am weary, almost asleep while writing this. All I can really think of is sleep – I don't know if I have ever felt so exhausted, ever. I was lifeless in the rain today, practically sliding on my walking poles into town. I wasn't physically pained, although we did climb a fair height. But I am overcome by the weight of it all, and in this moment I don't want to walk anymore. I am more sluggish than the dead snails in my pack. I want to stop. I want to cry. I want to go home. And when I go home I don't want to work. All I want is some rest.

Not a very energetic beginning for a polymath wannabe, but sometimes the first step is hibernation. Yes? Do you know that when bears hibernate they don't pee for four months? Maybe if I was a bear, Malakai wouldn't be so frustrated with me.

See you soon.

Love J.

16

OKAY,

Capture Cerberus, the three headed dog of Hades. If Hercules could do it then you will be a shoo-in.

You can deal with the lion and the hydra, etc. on the pilgrimage back.

peg.

Dear Peg:

MY DAY STARTED WITH ANGER at Malakai, who is hounding me.... "Who were you before you were a lawyer?" I thought: Well I'm more than just a lawyer. I am. I am. Everybody can see that. Except, you know, they can't. I don't show any of my other skills very visibly, if at all. Assuming that I have some left.

In my next life, I will be more like you – a lawyer with the ability to make maflingo piñatas for parties and the most scrumptious cakes in the whole universe. My children did not believe that these things could be embodied in one person, until they met you.

Grenadine sharks and Shirley Temples and more types of choco-late in one house than anyone could imagine possible.

I walked ahead. Malakai caught up. I walked ahead again. I wanted to be left alone. I had no good answers for her and didn't want to keep trying to explain things. Eventually I gave in and we walked together. The rest of the day revolved around discuss-ing and thinking about the impact of the thoughts of others on the way we choose to live our lives. The way the vampires rule. Demons in sheep's clothing. The mouse that can slide under the door, no matter how small the crack. The open space opened for others, not for the self.

DID YOU KNOW THAT THE reason Hercules had to capture Cerberus alive, without using weapons, was to atone for killing his own wife and children, after being driven insane by Hera, goddess of marriage? In addition to being the goddess of mar-riage, Hera was also the wicked stepmother of Hercules and rode in a wagon pulled by peacocks. She threw one of her own children from Mount Olympus and sent two serpents to kill Hercules when he was a baby. They say that the Milky Way is the result of Hera's breastmilk streaming across the sky after she realized she had been tricked by Zeus into nursing a child not her own. Those Greeks. Sheeesh. They made everything so complicated.

Never mind Hera's troubles. Today, I have felt judged and de-fined every step of the way with my child. I am angry with her for being so headstrong and for using a particular tone with me. I am weary and tired of the emotion and have told her to stop mock-ing me, stop demanding things from me, without being gentle in return.

This is my child I am talking about. I love her. She was and is my perfect baby girl. When she was finally born after such a long struggle, I woke up in the middle of the night and she was lying on me, staring up at me with her huge blue, two-day old eyes. Like a little duck, imprinting on me. Mommy. I will protect her, I thought. I will never hurt her, I thought. No-one will crush her spirit, I thought. There are times when I have failed miserably in all of these things.

And then, today, I left her behind. I left her for the first time on this walk of ours because I had had enough of raising her for today and I didn't want to hear anymore. I didn't have to hear it. And for God's sake, it could have been worse. She could have had Hera for a mother!

So, by choice, I walked alone until Malakai and I made up after a few hours. It's been a long walk, and so many steps day after day shakes things up and out. We have each walked alone a lot of the time. But there is a mother / daughter journey in the separateness. That is absolutely true.

I have been looking constantly for the statue of the three-headed dog on the Camino because I want to bring a picture back to show you that I captured Cerberus. I have not succeeded, although I think I came close. I took a picture of a three-headed something, carved in a coat of arms on a building in one of the towns we passed through. There was a For Sale sign on the building, and if I were insane I would think it a sign from heaven that my purpose in life is to throw it all away and run off to Spain, to open a vegan, foot-washing albergue. I won't do that – because, of course, I'm not insane – but it sure was a tempting thought.

The more I walk the more I remember that I have had some very content periods during long stretches of time alone – when I was a teenager, when I was pregnant and working in the Ecology Garden, in the middle of the night in my office with my thoughts, and here on this path. I like being alone. I love being in my office now, alone without staff. I dance in my office. I sing between the computers sometimes. I really, really like it. And it is only for this reason that I will not quit practising law at the end of this trip.

Honestly, if I had to go back to an office full of people depending on me to pay their mortgages, I would quit altogether. I have no doubt about that. For years I paid people to be around me all of the time, organizing my day for me, moving paper for me, and knowing the daily details of my life. I don't like practising law enough to ever do that again. Not that these weren't good people in real life. I just don't like the employer / employee / bitch boss relationship, that's all.

I can't remember if I found the three-headed thing on the building before or after I decided that I would not quit. Perhaps it was in the middle of this quiet internal debate. What I have realized here is that in becoming a "grown-up" I have robbed myself of my own company, which I sincerely enjoy.

And truly I can't bear the thought of what I would become if I let my days go on like this for another fifteen years — full of futile compromises and unnecessary wasting of my time. My siblings are falling like flies. My eyes don't react well to things that make me unhappy. So that clinches it for me. This profession of ours is too consumed with misery, and stress, and the worst of human emotions. I have been consumed with alleviating the misery and the stress and the worst of human emotions ten hours a day, on most days. I've had enough. It's not that I am not tough enough. But I have had enough. I have lost my thick skin and I have to scale this monster back. I'm also going to quit the part-time Master's degree. The world doesn't need any more blah, blah, blah.

And so, in response to your task, I suppose what I have captured here, on the Camino, is my self. Let's just call it Cerberus, captured from the gates of Hell. A Herculean task and I'm not going back there! Thanks.

As for the nine-headed Hydra and the Lion who fell from the moon, I have already decided that I will take most of a summer when the kids are at camp (perhaps next?) and walk the Camino Norte to Finisterre, in the shadow of St. Francis. I'm sure that will be enough time to take care of those two monsters, don't you?

Love J.

17

Hi Julie:

June 19th

DO YOU HAVE THE LEATHER thong yet? I also need to know how you want the claw oriented to your body. Drop over or give me a call.

June 24th

Task: To visualize world peace

See you this afternoon.

Enjoy your trip. Glenn

Dear Glenn:

I REALIZE NOW, OF COURSE, THAT you gave me two tasks without intending to. My first task was to find the leather thong, which I did not do before I left. But yes, I now have the leather thong, and the claw is perfectly oriented to my body. It was given to me by a man in Manjarin who cut it with his knife using the same motion, in the same way, as you had shown me in the shop. It was as though I was looking at your reflection. The whole time at Manjarin was like that. I can't wait to tell you about it when I get home because I know that you will smile your perfect smile and understand.

Malakai and I decided first thing this morning, in the albergue at Sarria, that your second task is just impossible. There are too many people to have world peace. Too many needs. Too many wants. Too many daily distractions and annoyances. And then there are the people who are just nuts.

We let people starve on the other side of the world without ever considering that they may be connected to us.

We persecute and prosecute people who have done nothing wrong except be vulnerable, or poor, or the wrong colour, or the wrong sex, or in the wrong place at the wrong time on the wrong side of power.

We rest on our petty grudges with each other, and gossip and destroy, and silence and hurt.

These are not things that go well with the idea of world peace. And this is the world, so there will be no peace. There never has been.

The Camino is now very busy because we are starting to approach Santiago. Upon arrival in Santiago, all pilgrims who have walked at least the last one hundred kilometers to the cathedral are entitled to their *Compostela*, the pilgrim's certificate of completion. And so the path is absolutely full of people, school groups, and cows. There is no peace here.

We finally met the other Canadian mother-and-daughter team today. We have been hearing about them and they have been hearing about us. A woman behind me said to her mother: "That's too funny!" and I knew immediately that she was Canadian. Her name is Juli and she is beautiful. Her mother, Suzanne, is sixty and beautiful as well. Suzanne and I spent time talking about motherhood and the inability of women to say "no" — perhaps for the sake of keeping the peace. That is the other problem with world peace, by the way.

I said to Suzanne today that I have felt rage and pain at how much I have limited myself, held myself back, while at the same time succeeding at substantially so much in objective terms — by the measure of other yardsticks, not my own.

We talked about the fact that nothing grows in a courtroom. The Rule of Law is the foundation of world peace, but judges commit the ultimate violence of the state — it is a violent act to lock a person in a cage, or to give someone's children to another family. This is what it is, regardless of whether it can be justified in some way. First and most fundamentally, the violence of this power must be acknowledged before it can be justified.

In my work, I participate in the ceremonies that permit this to happen and hope that it is all for a just result. Over time, it becomes clear in practice that this is not always the case, and it does not sit well with me. I do not want to be pessimistic. I would like to be a Pollyanna. I want to maintain the stance of the wide-eyed innocent. I want world peace. That is what I want.

Suzanne's view is that the inability to say "no" is a woman's disease until mid-life, and then it changes. That seems to be right in line with my life. Age forty, and saying "no" ferociously. That's me. My body had to say "no" first, and then I followed. A pain portal. The medicine comes first, then the journey, says Proud Woman.

I SPENT SOME TIME TODAY THINKING difficult thoughts about both of these things: world peace and the word "no." I think you know that when I was seventeen I left home to go on a cultural exchange through Canada World Youth to Pakistan — the whole point of this being to provide Canadian youth with "a unique experience to become a global citizen." The part of this that I considered deeply, today, was my relationship with my Pakistani counterpart, Farah. At the beginning of the program, we were assigned our "counterparts" and began to get to know each other. Farah and I liked each other. I very much liked Farah. She was kind and strong, older than me, and a national field-hockey player in Pakistan. We got along well.

Just as we were about to leave for the community where we would live and work in Canada for three months, my group leader took me for a long walk and asked me to switch counterparts with another Canadian girl who did not want to continue with the girl that she was with.

I was only seventeen then, but I knew myself and I knew my mind and, in retrospect, I was very strong-willed in my way. Like Malakai, I suspect. The group leader and I walked, and he talked at me. I asked why *I* should be asked to change something that was good rather than the other people involved finding a solution to *their* own problem. I did not want to lose Farah as my counterpart because I enjoyed her so much. I did not want to switch. Why should I? I stood my ground and things stayed as they were.

We moved to our community in July and lived with a farm family in a small town in southwestern Ontario. We worked at the local newspaper and rode our bikes in and out of town almost every day. There was a deep blue barn that marked the mid-way point into town, and we both loved the colour of that barn. The other participants were scattered in the village and on farms nearby. Farah and I shared a room. She was a lovely girl, with a sense of humour and endless patience. This was a good match for me, because I was, and am, not patient by nature, and Farah's presence forced patience upon me. I think she enjoyed me too because I was slightly more ferocious than she was used to.

One night in early September, she wanted to go out after dinner to visit with the other girls who were living and working on a tobacco farm across the highway and on the next concession. We had something happening the next day, and I was tired. I suggested to her that she not go. She wanted me to go with her, but I said "no." Farah left on her bike for a quick visit and said that she would be back soon. I can still hear her going out the door.

The call came from a family that lived on the highway. There had been an accident and we should come, they said. Farah had been killed. We went, in the van, to the highway where many people were already congregated. There was a car with a smashed windshield; we heard that the driver was a young girl driving off to university after the long weekend. Farah's bike was at the side of the road, beside a pool of blood. The ambulance had come and gone. And that was it.

Her funeral in Canada was strictly Muslim. She was washed by a group of strangers — Muslim women who lived in a nearby city — but was otherwise untouched. It was my first view of unaltered death, and it was clear that her neck had broken on the windshield, exactly where the windshield itself had been broken.

A month after Farah died, my father had a heart attack. I flew home to Thunder Bay for the weekend and I told him that I was not going back, I was not going to Pakistan, and I was not going anywhere, ever. My father pushed me out of his hospital room on the morning of my flight with his hands and one word: "Go!"

I continued on, quietly, and went to Pakistan without Farah. In Pakistan, I lived with another Canadian and Pakistani counterpart team — I was their third wheel. I worked in the girls' school and in the sugar-cane fields. The children called me *Baji-ji* (big sister), and a wise, twelve-year-old boy named Abas was my quiet friend.

In December, Farah's family in Lahore demanded to see me. They had made one request already, but no-one had told me. They wanted to see me alone, and now, looking back, I don't think any of the group leaders were happy about that. But I was glad to spend a day with them, and her father told me not to feel bad because if I had gone with her that night, we both would have died. Perhaps so. But it would have taken that much more time for me to tie my shoes. That much more time for me to get my bike and for us to get out the door. It would have taken enough time for the university student to have been long gone, down the highway and on with her life. Still, it was a kind and generous thing for her father to say.

What I did not tell her father, and what I have never said out loud, is that I was selfish in saying "No, I will not change because I am happy with this." It is not my fault that Farah is dead, but it is also not a big leap to see that had I not said "no," she would still be alive.

Isn't it odd and tragic what we carry without knowing it. Saying "no" is, for me, a selfish act. I used to know how to say "no" very well. But look at what happened. It's hard for me to think about. I have to stop.

As for world peace, really, Glenn — it is hard to have world peace when the man beside you in the albergue is snoring so loudly that other pilgrims quietly get up in the night and pinch his feet to make him stop. It just so happened that he was sleeping next to me. I hardly slept at all.

The Camino, from Sarria on, is crowded and noisy. We were told it would be like this. My feelings toward my fellow pilgrims has changed with the throng, the screaming children, the quasi–theme-park atmosphere. This is not Roncesvalles or the Manjarin albergue, that's for sure. There are no Gregorian chants here. It is English music, television in the common room, and noise and snoring and far too much humanity after so much solitude.

But then again, the people who have joined the Camino at Sarria are perhaps weeks behind me physically. They must be sore, and physically tired. I will try to remember this.

There are washing machines now, and people actually use them. It is discordant. It is not what it has been. The unwritten rules of the Camino are broken with the influx, so I have decided that I need to pass quickly through Santiago and somehow on to Finisterre. I don't want to be surrounded by people. There are too many people now.

But back to the task, because it is important. How can there be world peace with so many people?

Go solo. Peace is a solo journey. Isn't that true? I think it is. *First comes the medicine, then the journey.*

You have to take a sharp turn to the right and keep walking until empty.

Then, do no harm. Each person, do no harm.

Then, learn to love. Each person, love.

It is very personal.

It is one note.

It is universal.

I CAME TO THE END OF this day with the words of my Canadian walking companion held close — there are only two emotions on the Camino, fear and love. Is love measurable? Is there a vibration to it? Is there a sound? Do the whales sing it? Can we become resonant vessels too?

I want to be a whale. I want to sing. I want my voice to be part of a symphony, and it must, therefore, be simply what it is. I have no control over the rest. The rest doesn't matter.

Solo / Harmony / Symphony

I can work on harmony. I can choose to be with people with whom I can be whole. This is the answer to Meredith's task a few days ago, which I was at such a loss to answer. I'll have to tell her.

The symphony of the universe will take care of itself, I think. It is about resonance – this has been my word for something inexplicable since my spine started vibrating so constantly at Manjarin.

Do you think that there are energy vibrations at the earth's core? Do you think that the wind carries these things? Do you think that we are, ourselves, Chladni figures – frozen music? Are we infinite? Divine? Perhaps so, and the fact that we don't know this is the single reason why there cannot be world peace. Is that true? You play with ideas, Glenn. There is nothing that can't be figured out in your shop. Perhaps we can get you and me and my friend Garth together in the shop to see what we can figure out with your frequency generator. Wouldn't that be fun? Or crazy? I think it would be fun, even if it were crazy. I want to make voice figures.

Malakai thinks I'm losing it. But I'm not. I'm free-floating. She does not recognize this part of me. She wanted to know what I was before I became a lawyer, and I think she has perhaps gotten more than she bargained for. To annoy her today, I started to sing out loud: "This is the dawning of the Age of Aquarius." She didn't even think I was funny, silly girl. I thought I was funny. I was joking and I made myself laugh. I also thought to myself that I am so strong, I bet I could walk to Finisterre in my tan leather Hugo Boss knee-length boots, and then burn them on the beach on the pilgrim pyre. To Finisterre with her boots on, just like a good pilgrim.

I would probably get blisters, though, and they are indeed beautiful boots. I love my boots, but I love my hiking shoes more. And I especially love my socks. I am very, very protective of my socks. Undoubtedly, my socks would bring world peace if everyone had a pair.

Love J.

18

Hi Julie K.

I WANT YOU TO OBSERVE WINDOWS: colour, shape, texture, and where they are situated.

Re: homes? churches?

Hope you and your daughter have a good walk.

Lots of luck. Ross

Dear Ross:

I HAVE SAUNTERED TODAY, AND STOPPED a great deal. This is because I was looking at windows, as you said. And taking pictures. And contemplating. I moved along at a snail's pace and it was wonderful.

Today, with your task, you have given me a much-needed rest day. Rest for the weary, as they say. My body is strong and I have no pain, but in my heart and soul and mind I am tired. I can barely keep my eyes open.

I began the day by going to look at a beautiful rose window in Portomarin at the Iglesia de San Juan, built in the thirteenth century by the Knights of St. John. We stayed in Portomarin last night, and because of your task for today, I wanted to see the rose window before we moved on. There is no other church like this on the Camino, from what I have seen. I have a picture of it that I will show you. The rose window is magnificent, resting above the doorway where there are stone-carved demons devouring sinners — one eating a leg, another eating a whole body. The medieval churches are very dramatic in that way.

The meaning of the rose window is varied. The petals of the rose, geometric and perfect, were considered in medieval times to be equal paths to the Divine Centre — first Aphrodite, then the Virgin Mary. Every religion uses the circle as a symbol of sacred unity. The same geometric patterns are found in Islam and Celtic art. It is said that a deep emotional and spiritual chord is struck by the play of light that passes through the glass of a rose window. Medieval alchemists said that a rose window, essentially a dodecahedron and a symbol connected with ether, had a transformative effect on the contemplator by permitting an altered state of perception in the light that it cast. A mandala, as in Eastern philosophy and religion.

In medieval cathedrals, every aspect of the building was considered with reference to the so-called divine proportions, following the principles outlined by the master-builder of Chartres in 1194. Mathematics made beautiful. Every space in the rose window at San Juan is defined by another, smaller geometric figure, all relative to the centre. The twelve major divisions of the rose window are thought to point to the finite and infinite, earth and heaven, matter and spirit.

My mother's name was Rose.

Thank you for giving me this task, Ross. I have thought of your whole family today from here, so far away from home. I have said to you often that your parents must have been wonderful people to have raised such a brood. It is a fact that I have been blessed with your particular knock at my door on your way to do your downtown business. You all share the same smile, the same laugh, and the same easy generosity of spirit. These qualities are rare, and not often found so close in such numbers, as it is with your extended clan. I am lucky.

I KNOW THAT YOU MISS JOAN. I also know that you know that a long life means that so much is sure to come. These things are most definitely some of the things that I have been thinking of through my time on the Camino. It is about finding the points between what is finite and what is infinite, between what is matter and what is spirit. Where is the window to the spirit, the soul? I hadn't considered windows as part of this before today. I have cried a lot of tears here, looking for that window. I don't have the answer yet, Ross. And I am sorry for that.

I am so weary that I can barely write another word. We will have to have a long sit on your porch, and perhaps a long walk on the jail hill and see if we can figure it all out. Can we do that?

Love J.

19

I "THINK" I UNDERSTAND YOUR REQUEST. lets see, here is my request. when walking look up. i mean, look forward and not down to the ground. as a matter of fact, try looking two feet higher than your own height. that is my request. i suggest this as i remember you most as someone who most often walks with her head down. hope this is what you are looking for. sylvia

ARZUA, JULY 20, 2009

Dear Sylvia:

I THOUGHT OF YOU MUCH EARLIER on the path, when my back was so sore and my pack was so heavy. I wrote a letter to another friend, on one of the first days filled with physical pain, about how little I was looking forward to the anticipated failure of this nineteenth day. I had tested myself, and I was completely incapable of looking up with my pack on my back.

I thought of you again a few days later as I was walking under a highway overpass and heard music being played for the passing pilgrims by two men standing outside of their car with their instruments. Overhead, there were two pairs of shoes dangling on the power lines over the highway. I was, obviously, able look up on that day – a small improvement – and I took a picture of the shoes. You and I discussed the meaning of shoes on a wire on the way to Keene just before I left, which is why it made me think of you. I have never seen women's shoes on a power line. I wonder why?

Those days feel like they were months ago – I have taken so many steps and had so many thoughts since then. Rhythmic and disorganized thoughts, from my free-floating mind. My letters are getting shorter, because I have entered some sort of walking meditation through the day. I have found that at the end of the past couple of days I have very few perceptible thoughts about anything at all. My brain is empty.

At dinner last night, with Canadians we have met, there was much talk about the limits of our mind and the control of the right brain by the left. All of the lists and all of the details and all of my organizing of myself have felt so irrelevant as I walk. I can now easily slip into only my breath. Not only that, but I can enjoy it. I have calmed the monkey-brain and I'm not sure where my mind is half the time, when I'm walking alone. And I am not bored. But I also don't have a lot of interesting things to write to you about today.

Here is the amazing thing. You wanted me to look up while walking, and today I did, all day. Way up, like *The Friendly Giant* – did you watch that show? Two feet above my head, as you said.

I stopped for my morning coffee, took off my pack, and relaxed for a bit. When I was finished I threw on my pack and continued, happily striding along with my walking poles and looking up. The trees were filled with birds, and I listened and watched for them. I had been going along like this for at least two hours, thinking God knows what, when I realized that I had not closed the chest-fasteners on my pack. This means that not only was I looking way up, doing what I had previously considered impossible, but I had nothing to support my pack other than my own strong shoulders with all of the weight hanging straight down from me. I felt no pain. I did not feel my pack at all, frankly.

There are a lot of people on the path now, because this is the busy and frenetic stretch of the Camino. Last night at dinner, there was complaining of the intrusion of all of these other people into the solitude and quiet pace that we have become so used to. Because of all of the talk about right brain / left brain, I thought that this was a good metaphor for the left brain intruding on the present-moment thinking of the right. I was also thinking of something I wrote early on in the path about taking a sharp turn to the right at one point in the Camino, following Malakai's blue bandana. Metaphorically speaking, this is indeed what I have done — I have taken a sharp turn into my right brain and continued on from there.

But today the path was filled with all of these people, and their chatter, disturbing the beauty and wholeness and solitude. For the first time, while walking, I pulled out my iPod and put on my earphones because I did not want to hear the constant hum of other people. Malakai went on ahead. I wanted to listen to Oliver Schroer and to my Tibetan singing bowls, and that is what I did. I bought raspberries at the side of the path and was happy in my little bubble, staring ahead and up at the trees and the sky-blue sky.

At some point I was walking at such a clip that I decided that I should listen to my Queen playlist. I hadn't listened to it since the train on the way to Bayonne. I moved along, passing pilgrims and creating my own space, and dancing to Queen as I went. I looked above the heads of all of the people who might have annoyed me otherwise. I couldn't see them and I couldn't hear them. They didn't matter, and I couldn't care less what any of them thought of me, bopping along the Camino. I had no interest in them and there was nothing to complain about.

I played with my poles, looking up at them as I swung them in the air, almost running with my strong, strong legs. I moved so fast and so far that I left all of the people behind. At some point I was on the path completely alone and very proud that I had beaten them all – to where I didn't know.

I came into a small village, surprised that there was not a café or place to go to the bathroom. I continued along the road for a while, enjoying my solitude and my music, until I was stopped by a farmer on his tractor. He asked me, in Spanish, if I was walking the Camino. I pulled my earphones out so that I could hear him and said yes, I was. A happy and proud pilgrim.

This kind man informed me that I was about five kilometres off the path. I had been looking up and had missed the yellow arrow.

And so I had to turn around and go back five kilometres. I was not sad. I laughed because I had been lost in never-never land – looking up into the sky, without a care in the world, and without a catalogue of any of my thoughts. I had been in a reverie all day. I had remained entirely connected, with my eyes and my thoughts, to something higher than all of the people, all day.

Not to mention the fact that I had been totally and completely lost.

When I finally met Malakai in the town where we were staying, I had walked forty-two kilometres and was ecstatic with my health on this day. And my calm state in my long and lost walking mediation – eyes forward and up, like the cat pose. Thank you.

Love J.

20

"IN ORDER TO COME BACK to the present moment, we must consciously slow our minds. To do this, first decide you are not in a hurry. Your left mind may be rushing, thinking, deliberating, and analyzing, but your right mind is very m-e-l-l-o-w."

Jill Bolte Taylor, Ph.D
from her book *My Stroke of Insight*

Task is ... be mellow
Janette

Dear Janette:
I HAVE TODAY, I THINK, MADE the decision to go on to Finisterre. We were up at 4:00 a.m. and started walking because we wanted to make it to Santiago today. We weren't able to eat, so it was a different start from what we are used to, with toast and lingering over coffee. We have not been in a rush thus far to get out before the hoard. But things are different now. This day we were up before the roosters and out into the dark, realizing

slightly too late that we had sent the head lamp on to Santiago. Rapidly into the forest and the darkness, lit only by Malakai's iPod screen, it was frightening and we had not planned ahead for food. My platypus was blocked so I also had no water. My task was to remain *mellow* in this — as my body was filled with panic — no food, no water, no light.

We were joined by two men who had been walking since the first of June from Toulouse — they were known by reputation along the way as serious walkers, up before dawn. We were ahead of them — super pilgrims we were on this day. Still behind them was the man from Montreal who has walked more than forty-five kilometres per day and brags that he has spent more at the pharmacy tending to his feet than he has on food.

We found our way at a crossing with their help, and then carried on. Malakai descended into hunger and tiredness and, in her delirium, said many things to me that if she were older than seventeen she might regret someday. But, being still a teenager has benefits that she does not yet appreciate — one of which is eventual forgiveness for pointed adolescent words. If only it worked the other way....

I said to George later that he would have been very proud of my calm fortitude in the face of this final day and all of the words it contained, as we made our way toward Santiago. I think that by the time we had reached the cathedral at 5:00 p.m., we had walked for eleven hours and over fifty kilometres. I had been verbally tested and tried by Malakai more so than on any other day. I promised her today that we will come back when she is forty and I am sixty-three, and I mean it.

Calm is not my first state of being. This is obvious to all, including me. But today I was indeed calm. I was also totally and completely amazed when I re-read your task at the end of the day

— having acted only on my memory of it in the early morning —
to discover that your quotation was from *A Stroke of Insight*, which
we happened to be discussing at some length at dinner last night
with some new friends. This is my life here: one of complete and
total synchronicity now that I have gotten out of my own way.
That is how it has felt — even the parts that have caused me to cry
uncontrollably and beat my walking poles against the dirt and
yell at my beautiful daughter when she has said things that are
difficult to hear, or when she has said things, as she did today, that
she ought not to have said. Being hungry and tired is no excuse,
for either of us.

I have been quietly walking most of the time and paying attention to my days as they pass, and to my life as it moves through
me. I have returned to this many times in the evening as I write
my letters, and have considered your part in it. You did yoga with
me. You made me make the stupid "Oooommmmmm" sound
and showed me what the vibration felt like by asking me to put
my hand on your back.

At the Millbrook Film Festival years ago I said thank you, and
I will say it again in this letter, again through my tears, for the
magic that you somehow opened in me. You have no idea — perhaps you do, but I doubt it. Because it's not about you. It's about
the power of the universe moving through you and moving into
me. That is what love is — that is what it feels like, and that is
what it does.

I have returned, finally, to the realization that the vibration in
my spine is a continuation of what I felt that first day on the floor
in my office. It is not a neurological disease. It will not kill me.
It is the sound of my brother's fistula. It is the sound of life. It is
the sound of the "oooommmmmm" in your back. It is like the

whale's song. It is my life, moving through me and around me. It is my spine, my core, singing to me.

It was only supposed to be about yoga, remember? "Hi, Janette, can you teach me how to move my spine so that it won't turn into bamboo, like it says in the books?"

I'm not fusing yet. I'm walking the Camino. I'm not sure what to do about the autoimmune disease but it appears that I'm doing something right this month in spite of it.

And so I need to tell you once again that I love what you brought into my life. I love the way you say "Breathe...." and the way you say "ankle bones." Thank you.

Love J.

21

YOUR TASK IS TO THINK about nothing for the entire day – clear your mind of the running thoughts. You must be completely in the moment. You must not think about work, your relationships, your family, your problems, but to focus on the steps that you are taking, the sounds that you are hearing, the smells that you are smelling and the things that you are seeing. You must focus your mind on your present experience without being drawn to the greater implications of your journey on your existence.

Have a great trip!

Suzan

Dear Suzan:

TODAY I AM IN SANTIAGO, very, very far from where I started, and very, very far from home.

This is my second day of being tasked with "mellowness," and I am getting the hang of it after all of these steps. What has been interesting about this day is that I have been occupied with your task while being here in this large, frenetic city during a festival.

We are staying in a small hotel very close to the cathedral and there are people, and scallop shells, everywhere. There is also music and noise and motor vehicles. So many wheels on things. After so many days of quiet walking, it is hard to be in the moment. Being in the moment means taking all of this in, and there is a lot of it.

Malakai and I spent much of the day apart, and I wandered through the streets alone, in the rain. Over this past month, it has rained only once, briefly, while walking through Galicia. As we approached the cathedral yesterday, the skies opened and it has been raining ever since. The poor pilgrims who didn't press on yesterday are arriving today in a full downpour. The steps of the cathedral are full of umbrellas and ponchos. I have a big red poncho which Malakai thinks makes me look very silly. She bought a perfect purple umbrella.

I have one blister, on my big toe, and it hurts. Here in the city, I feel like a wimpy tourist with my limp and my blister. On the path, it was different.

I ate alone in a café this morning and drank coffee and ate white Wonder bread toast. I loved it. I read the whole newspaper in Spanish and sort of figured out a few things that are going on in the world. I was fascinated by the fact that I understood almost every fifth word, simply the result of walking through this language. It was a very slow, leisurely breakfast. There is no reason not to have such languor at home, but it's something that I always feel guilty for wanting outside of vacation-time. When I am home, I will try very hard to lounge over *The Globe and Mail* and read it with purpose, like I did today. Usually I just skim the headlines, speed-read things that catch my eye, become instantly annoyed with the world, and get going.

I went shopping. I went to the bank. I don't do these things alone very often. Errand running is usually something we do as a group in my house. It's more efficient that way. Rarely do I walk down any street and window-shop in the middle of a day. People in Spain appear to do it quite happily, all of the time. And then they work. And then they have an afternoon nap. And then they work a little bit more. And then the streets come alive in a meandering way. Not like the multidirectional crossing of the four corners at Yonge and Dundas. Very different from that.

I went to the bank and am amazed that after a month away there is still some money left. There is a computer place around the corner from the hotel and I spent some time there because I wanted to check a couple of things on the Internet. I did check my email and logged in briefly to the office. I know you told me specifically not to do this — but what was interesting about it was that I truly did not care. What I was reading about, back home on my office server, (a) was not earth-shattering and (b) appeared to have very little impact on my existence. Reading quickly through the correspondence that had come in, and the mountain of emails, I was weirdly relaxed and felt very much as though I was doing nothing.

It made me think of my friend Joanne, who died about six years ago. She was a legal assistant in the office where I articled and was diagnosed with cancer shortly after I was called to the Bar. She was a very good friend to me, very mothering and loving. She absolutely adored George and was always full of good advice, like "you have to marry that man!" It took a long time for George and me to actually get married, but when we did, Joanne found it very exciting and was at the house in full force wearing a beautiful big hat.

When she was dying, I put off going to visit her until it was almost the end. I was told to go sooner but I didn't, and by the time I visited she was already slipping into a very deep slumber. I was alone in her room with her and had things I needed to tell her, which I did, to her closed eyes and still face. I was so angry at myself for waiting so long, and so frustrated that she couldn't hear me, that I said at one point, "Goddammit, open your eyes!" What a thing to say to a dying woman. But she did open her eyes, full of tears, and looked at me, and said, "I heard you." I was so glad. Then, because she was awake, George came in and we had a very, very short visit. The last thing she said to me, with a smile, as she was drifting back to sleep was "Go fiddle, or do whatever it is that you do."

Go fiddle. Do whatever it is that you do. How's that for perspective? At the point of death, it appears clear that most of the ways that life is spent comes down to just fiddling. All of the things that are so important, and all of the ways in which people are so self-important, mean very, very little. A speck of dust. A spark of light. That's it.

The fiddling had better be fun, that's all I can say. And if it's not fun, it had better be worth it.

I watched people today, as I had these thoughts. I tried to pay close attention to their faces and tried to read their emotions, since I could not understand their language. The most visibly happy people I saw were the street musicians, the lady selling cheese in a very small shop, and grandparents – particularly grandfathers with their grandchildren.

Malakai and I walked through a very strange little village the other day that appeared to have only three living residents in it. The first person we came across was holding a hose and spraying water on the garbage can across the street and the weeds beside it. He was very much enjoying this job and was so completely "in the moment" that he didn't notice us waiting for several minutes. We had to wait for him to stop watering so that we could pass, and eventually he did, with a smile. The next person we encountered was a tiny gnome-like woman with a huge nose who popped out of the doorway of her house with sugar-coated crepes for us. We had to pay for them, and she didn't think that we paid her enough when I gave her the change that I had readily accessible. This led to scrambling through our packs for more change with a total payment of over four euros. The happiness this produced resulted in our being given two more crepes. I have no idea what language this woman was speaking, but her emotions were very clear. The last resident was a man who was digging a trench in the sand outside his doorway with his foot, so that the rain would run away from the house. All three people appeared to be about a hundred-and-four years old, and all were completely enraptured by the very simple activities they were engaged in.

I'm not sure if it was the same day, or another, when we came upon a memorial on the path with a piece of writing attached to it. There are many memorials along the way, for people who have died while walking the Camino. Some have simply collapsed. Others have been hit by cars or suffered some other tragedy. This particular memorial was for a woman, and I should have stopped to copy what was written, it moved me so. I can't now remember the words, but the meaning was that before you produce anything – a piece of music, a piece of art, a piece of writing – you must live the daily, simple things of life. You must tend a garden, cook food, clean, live, and then pour the life out onto the page, into the music, onto the canvas. I am paraphrasing, but that is what I remember from it. I keep returning to a short conversation that I had a with a young German girl at the beginning about deciding what to keep carrying in our packs after walking for a couple of days with the weight of it. She said that in order to understand the need, you first need to have the experience. As I was reading the memorial, I thought that it was the same thing. The creative life comes from life. Life comes first.

I am not good at all of those domestic things. I have gone through short phases of domesticity – I sewed cloth diapers, I made my own baby food, I have made wild grape jelly exactly twice, I binge clean and purge to the complete dismay of my husband and children. I have no domestic routines. I have no annual domestic events, although the making and canning of wild grape jelly should really be an annual event because it is such a dramatically purple thing to do. I do not cook. I barely do laundry – I can do it well, but never consistently. I hate pulling hair from the bathtub drain. I hate the corners in the backs of the cupboards more than anything in the world. George, on the other hand, is always happy after he cleans the fridge.

I should try being "in the moment" when I vacuum, which is a rare event. Maybe it would help. Maybe if I could groove to the zen of vacuuming, I would do it more and therefore have more clean, clear surfaces in my life. That would be nice. But first I have to spend less time working, and actually value the time spent not working. This means valuing the other parts of life that should come first.

But for now, I really have nothing to do but finish writing to you and go to sleep. That's very nice.

Love J.

22

OK, JULIE. YOUR MISSION, SHOULD you choose to accept it, is the following:

Pick an animal; any animal. It can be something as familiar as your personal dog or unfamiliar, like a wild animal – a bird or deer or whatever you like. For one day – or any part thereof – you must view the world as if you were that animal. What would make you happy? What would scare you? What would be something that you would be drawn toward or stay away from?

When you eat, you should eat something that animal would also eat. If a dog or cat, eat meat. If a bird, only grain, fruit or insects (ha!). If a deer, just greens. Keep an eye out for enemies. Nap in the shade, if necessary. Breed if it's mating season (sorry, George).

Suggestions: Don't be a nocturnal animal like a raccoon. Don't be a deer if it's hunting season.

Have a great trip and let me know what you end up being and how it turns out.

Buen viaje amiga!

Evelyn

Dear Evelyn:

THIS IS A VERY INTERESTING task for me, and when I tell
you why, I wonder what you will think. It's not every day (or ever,
really) that I say out loud what I am about to say out loud – and
that is that I have animals that follow me and there are faces in
the trees.

When I was about twenty-five, I met a woman who gave me a
hawk feather. I lost it after a few years and have felt bad about it
ever since. But I remember George running into the house one day
when we still lived in Peterborough: there were five hawks circling
the house where I had been sitting and working. I thought it odd,
and beautiful – as did he, or else he wouldn't have run so fast to
pull me outside to show me. This went along with a number of
other things about the woman who gave me the feather, and the
things that she told me, way back then. It's a long story.

Around the time my dad came to Millbrook, a heron started
showing up. Really showing up – like flying directly in front of my
truck, centred in the windshield, leading me down the highway. It
always appeared when there was a decision to be made about my
dad that I didn't want to make, or difficult family things that I
didn't want to face or deal with. I whispered this quietly to a friend
once and he asked me, out loud, if I was having a nice talk with my
mother. An odd thing to say.

When my dad finally moved to Centennial Place, the nurse was
so pleased that he had been assigned the room that he now lives
in, because it overlooks the pond and there had often been a heron
that stood on the chain-link fence looking into the window of
that room. The nurse gave my dad a picture of the heron. The
heron only came back once after he moved in – on the evening
before his eightieth birthday. My dad went to the window, looked

out with bright eyes, and said, "Well, there..."

When my brother was sick and at my house after his kidney transplant, six deer crossed the road in front of me one day. The deer were magnificent, and there were so many. I returned home and burst into the kitchen to tell him about them. After Kevin died, I went to Thunder Bay and found myself standing outside the hotel for a long time talking to a deer that was in the small strip of bush between the hotel and the Trans-Canada Highway. Imagine talking out loud to a deer like that, but that is what I did.

Then before we left for home, after the funeral, we went to my mother's grave, where there were three fresh and steaming mounds of deer poop on her grave-plaque in the ground. I drove alone to get gasoline after that and rolled down the windows, screaming to the sky, "Okay! Okay!" And then I forgot. Or talked myself away from it. And life goes on.

But in February I saw the woman who had given me the hawk feather. Again it's a long story, but I found her after fifteen years because of something said to me the day after my brother's funeral. Her name is Proud Woman, and this time she gave me a bear claw and some stones. And a promise that we would go to the forest for a weekend before the summer is done.

When you read my letter to Tama, which I will give to you, you will see what happened to me and to my bear claw on that day at a place called Manjarin.

I have also been carrying my flute with me, which I got from the woman with the drums to whom I sent your peacock feather. It was while driving home after that cruise in March that I had an experience where the trees for miles all had faces - in great detail with wrinkles on the faces and folds in the clothing of the people in the trees. Very strange stuff, I know.

So in the telling of this I have, for all intents and purposes, gone completely and totally woo-woo on this day, Day "V." Herons and hawks and deer and bear claws and peacock feathers. To write it all on one page is a bit much, but I am tired of being afraid of being known. And so I have decided here, on this path, that I will no longer hide myself, or morph myself, or have myself sucked out of me. I will be more as I have been here. I will not be afraid.

So what that I have crazy things happening in my life that make me feel sometimes that I am losing my mind? Am I the only one? I can't be. Gosh, I hope not. Because really, it is so strange and exciting and perfect and wonderful. I want to shout from the top of a mountain, "Look, look, open your eyes! Look at what is there!" There is so, so much more to us than we allow. St. Francis of Assisi, the patron saint of my first day on the Camino, was also the patron saint of the animals. That must count for something!

BUT ASIDE FROM ALL OF that, my very real experience of this day was of being alone in my small hotel room, growling for most of the day. When I woke, I of course decided to be a bear. I told Malakai that I needed to eat nuts and berries and seeds all day. I sent her out to the fruit market to find some berries, and I went into the bath. It was hardly bear-like to send my daughter out to forage for me, but that was what I did.

I had earlier thought that I would spend this day walking to Finisterre alone but had decided already that I would not go. I chose instead to stay with Malakai, but I really only came to this decision after having a long hot bath upon arriving in Santiago. If I walk the Camino again, I will remember that it is very important to stay away from all bathtubs unless you want to be knocked off your course.

But it's a good thing that I decided to stay. Had I been on the path, I would have had to crawl into a cave, because today I got my period and it came with such force that I was in bed all day. Hibernating and growling like a bear. That was a surprise, and not what I had imagined your task to be when I woke up!

I have a difficult menstrual cycle. Before, during, and after — my personal "curse" is very difficult, and always has been. In all the time I have been practising law, it is only by the grace of God or some other luck that I have never turned green and fainted in a courtroom, mid-argument. I have turned green in almost every other context. I spent a birthday dinner out in the back seat of the car, moaning, while my family ate the rest of the meal inside the restaurant. My wonderful landlords have picked me up off the floor in my office, I think more than once. I have been on the floor, in the front hall, in the middle of the night, not able to move. I think on that particular occasion George came downstairs and stepped over me, saying, "Oh my God, it's only your period!" Men don't get it at all — even my husband, who is among the most sensitive souls alive, in his peculiar way.

I fainted in sex-ed in grade five. Perhaps it was because I intuitively knew what was coming for me. The public-health nurse put up the black-and-white diagram of a uterus, with drops of blood coming out the magic-marker vagina, and I turned green and fainted. I woke up, on the floor, screaming and covered in sweat. Imagine the horror! I have searched my whole life to find someone else who fainted in sex-ed. So far, it's been only me.

I also fainted several times in pre-puberty while looking up "menstruation" in the medical encyclopedia. Having fainted already, I wanted to know everything about it so that I could be prepared. The problem was that at the same time, my mother was dying. So I would sit in the chair in the living room and read the sections on "cancer" and "tumour" and "brain," and then flip to "menstruation." Inevitably, I would get up and pass out. I passed out in this way while walking to the kitchen and hit my head on the dishwasher. I also passed out in the bathroom and hit my head on the toilet. I have always been completely ridiculous in some ways. This is one of them.

And so today I was pathetic and ridiculous – writhing in pain on the hotel bed. Malakai came back (without fruit), took one look at me, and said, basically, "Oh dear, well I'll be going then." I needed fruit, I said. I had to be a bear and I needed fruit. She still left.

I am a mother bear. I am not maternal, or domestic. But I am fierce. And a protector. I know that. And I think that perhaps my children know that too. Anyone who has known us for more than ten years knows something of this.

When I have my period, the first four hours are like full labour. I sweat and ache and throb and, sometimes, vomit. It's a terrible monthly routine and I have said to George that I would very much like to take out my uterus and stick it on a shelf where it can simply be worshipped from afar, instead of this horrific monthly power that I must bow to. In fact, I have asked for this to happen, but apparently you are not entitled to a hysterectomy just because you are sick and tired of being a girl. People can have gender re-assignment surgery, but I can't decide when and how to get rid of my uterus? How is that fair? The option that was provided to me was to microwave my uterus – frying it so that it would be just dead up there. I can't do that. Besides, they have to give you a month of drugs that put you into quasi-menopause first, and I'm quite sure that I would kill someone. I also can't go off my heavy-duty anti-inflammatories that keep my eyes in check, in order to take some other wonder drug.

So I suffer, month by month. I have "Free and Easy Wanderer" pills from the naturopath. I think they help a little. I like being a free and easy wanderer.

But today was so awful that all I could do was put on my iPhone and rock in my bed. First I tried Oliver Schroer, but the violin was too grating. I settled on the Buddhist singing-bowl tape from my acupuncturist and really tried to listen, because Agda's task to me has been to isolate one note. I focused with all of my might. And it was very strange.

My throat closed, which was a frightening feeling. I have not felt that before and I couldn't make it stop. Because my throat was closing, I found myself starting to growl, deep in my throat. I growled as I rocked and listened to the vibrating bowls and went off somewhere, beyond the pain. I put the iPhone on "repeat" and went in and out of sleep for hours.

WHEN I THOUGHT OF IT later, it reminded me of labouring before Malakai was born — all night, alone in the bathtub, moaning and growling and rocking the pain in the water, in the dark. When Malakai was born, it took too long and hurt way too much. I listened to the midwife and to her father, neither of whom knew what they were talking about, and I laboured in their company — utterly and completely alone — for fifty-two hours. For what?

The late eighties and early nineties, at least at Trent and in Peterborough, were full of endless falafel and taboulleh potlucks and wymyn, some of whom gathered in "covens." I have run as far as I could from the drivel that went along with being that young and pseudo-confident. Natural childbirth was part of the whole deal. I laboured for fifty-two hours with Malakai before having a caesarean section. She came out with a cone-head to the ceiling because she had been trapped in my pelvis for that whole time, and yet at the next year's midwifery picnic I was roundly chastised for not having "tried hard enough." Can you believe it?

Anyway, today I did basically the same thing, because period pain and labour pain come from the same starting point, and I didn't stop this until Malakai came in several hours later. By that time I could move again, and the pain in my uterus was just a dull achy afterthought.

What a strange letter to write. "Dear Evelyn: On your day, I decided to be a bear and did nothing but hibernate, menstruate, and growl to keep my throat from closing." But that is what happened. And it was, in its odd way, as wonderful as all of the other days that I have spent on the Camino. Now that I can move again.

Perhaps when I come home, I will have to build a menstrual hut where I can go to growl alone at the moon, instead of at my husband. I resist all that witchy wymyn stuff with all my might, but there is no doubt that there are things that only women can understand. Please tell me that menopause will not be like this every day, all day.

Love J.

23

THE "W" TASK! IF WE'RE counting right, this must be day twenty-three of your trip. You've been tasked to death and here's one more.

You've walked so many steps, seen so much, thought so much and now...

Think of your adventure as colour.

Simply become aware of the colours surrounding you and take away from all this that on this day, you're looking at the world through the eyes of an artist – a colourist at that.

Make it fun and happy trails...

Joe & Murielle

FINISTERRE, JULY 24, 2009

Dear Joe and Murielle:

I AM IN FINISTERRE, AT THE end of the world, with a hotel room of my own, with a double bed and a balcony opening onto the bluest blue and the reddest red of the harbour.

Malakai wanted Wi-Fi, in a room at a hotel akin to a Holiday Inn that opened onto a construction site. I wanted the rickety balcony on the fourth floor of a hostel with a view of the harbour. I decided that I was entitled to this because my day was intended by you to be focused on colour, and I could not be an artist without a view. Instead of fighting about it, I left Malakai in the Wi-Fi room and checked myself into the hostel down the road. I was selfish. I said "no." I took time and space. We are near the end of the journey, and money is tight, but I did it anyway. I chose to be close to beauty. I decided that I had a choice. Or had no choice. Because of your task, this is what was required.

Staying in separate hotels created a distance, so Malakai and I had to plan to meet for dinner. That was fun. She had been to the beach and I had done other things. I had a lovely lunch alone, I watched the water, I wrote, I wondered about things to myself.

You have suggested to me that I might feel my way beyond my words — to a place of colour and sensation in an unused part of my mind. I have not known that place. I have only known words.

But it is truly impossible to catalogue all of the colours and shapes of the ocean. As I watched it, it appeared to be as alive and as eternally changeable as, in fact, it is. There are no words.

From the ocean at Finisterre, it is a short climb to the blue of the sky, broken only by the ridged hills, partially hidden by silver mist. The mist is the same colour as the gulls that sit on the roof outside my balcony. It is a red clay-tile roof, weathered orange with large patches of green moss.

I am glad to have my own balcony and the quiet of my own thoughts. Here, from my balcony, the fishing boats sit on the water in primary colours. The light of the sun crests on the waves and beats against the textured rooftop. The clay tiles are covered in dusty birds' feathers, beside where I sit.

I am up high and I can see. My eyes do not hurt, even in the hot sun, and they are wide, wide open. That is the result of a month of walking. I have clear, clear eyes. It's so wonderful to be able to see so easily. Nothing in my body is causing me pain today except the blister on my left big toe, which is angry and light purple. I had not, before today, considered the colour of my blister.

Your task feels romantic to me – a much softer way to spend time than I usually do. I think I have been spending far too much time trying to become hard enough to absorb the things that repel me in my work. I am not, by nature, hard. I find these things hard, but I myself am not.

I am soft. Agda's task has required me to live, for a few moments each day, in a soft container of my own choosing. I have chosen an egg filled with sky-blue. I have been able to hold this one colour in my mind, in my egg, because it is the colour of the whole creation of sky around me as I walk through my days. This is a colour I have come to know well.

When I close my eyes and turn to Agda's task each day – for hers was a daily task – I am now able to imagine the whole of the universe, the whole of the sky, inside my small space. I am able to keep it for myself in those few moments, contained only by my mind and subsumed inside my body.

And I think that the reverse can also be true. I really do. Joe, we have all seen your huge, exuberant spirit burst into the world around you, beyond your physical body, regardless of the day. When you enter a room, the contours change and the room is fuller than could ever be imagined. The full spectrum of colour moves from the inside out. It's true.

Love J.

24

CREATE SOMETHING WITH MALAKAI
Sue.

Dear Sue:

I AM SUPPOSED TO CREATE SOMETHING today with
Malakai, you said. But again we have gone our separate ways at
the Cabo Finisterre, because she was hungry and I have no patience left. I want to be alone. I want to break free of the constant
negotiation of needs. I am angry with her today and silently tired
of being a mother, although I do love her so. I want her just to pay
for her own lunch and let me be. Baby birds are just kicked out of
the nest, and that's it. Birds don't cling and fuss and guilt like we
do. They are slick and decisive. That is what birds are.

I am not a bird. I am a mother. A mother bear, if anything. But
I have checked myself into my own hotel room in Finisterre and I
am happy. I am not justifying my every breath to the child that I
created, and I'm learning a staggering lesson from this. If I'm able
to separate myself from my child, then my long-entrenched self /

non-self confusion with the rest of the world should be a piece of cake. I'm going to hope for that anyway.

I wrote this to you this morning, and as I finish I can tell you that today was a truly incredible day in its ending. After Malakai left me at the lighthouse, I spoke briefly with an artist from whom I bought a card with an "M" and a butterfly. I will frame it for Malakai with her Compostela, someday soon. I had better not lose it, because what I plan to do is a very nice thought. I often have very nice thoughts and plan to do nice things, and then I don't. The result is that my nice thoughts stay only in me. The love doesn't flow out as it should. It gets stuck.

I asked the artist how people get back to town after watching the sunset at the Cabo Finisterre, because the road is so treacherous. She drew me a map to a beach on the other side of town and told me that no-one knew that this was the place to go.

As I walked back to town, I passed a café and saw a South African woman and her young son having lunch. We had thought we had lost them several days back, so I was very happy to see them again. We sat all afternoon and shared stories. I told them about a place called Manjarin and the people I had met there, including an Italian. They had a story about an Italian too. At the end of a long and leisurely afternoon, we decided that we would have dinner and go to watch the sunset together. I promised to bring my camera so that we could see whether we were speaking about the same Italian.

I left them and walked alone to try to find the artist's beach so that we would know where to go. I indeed found the entrance to the boardwalk that led to the beach, though I didn't walk all the way down before dinner. As I was walking back to town and toward my hotel, I saw a familiar face coming toward me on the street. It was the Italian, whom I hadn't seen since Manjarin. He was so happy to see me, and I him. He ran across the street to hug me and I decided, in that moment, that every friendship should have this quality of joy, without language. Because, of course, the Italian and I have never spoken. We have only been in each other's company. He soon went on his way and I did not see him again.

I found Malakai and the South Africans and we had a wonderful dinner, full of chatting and laughter. I confirmed, with my camera, that the Italian and my story and that in the South African story were one and the same. We lingered and left late to saunter down to the beach. As we walked, it became clear that we had to hurry. As we started down the boardwalk – which was much longer than we expected – something in the light changed and I started to run and laugh, and run faster. I had never run like that before. I yelled to them that we had to run to catch the sun. This made me laugh more. There was a mountain in the way, and we couldn't see the sun. And the light was moving. I ran hard until I came past the mountain to the point where we would see and arrived just as the sun hit the lip of the water at the horizon.

I have never had such a feeling of joy and confirmation and grace. I burst. It was the perfect end to the day, our last day in Finisterre. I was watching the sun fall at the edge of the world. For that is what it was. It was not a sunset. A sunset is meek. This was a sunfall. It sank heavily into the water, and within only a minute or two it was gone.

The light that lingered as the moon rose was spectacular, and I kicked off my shoes to run to the water. I was alone, with waves crashing, for a long time. I cried to the ocean and I felt larger than life, far beyond the edges of my own body. I can't explain it, Sue. The ocean was filled with the sound of my brother's fistula. It was the reverse of what happened when he put my head on his arm so long ago, it seems, and I heard the sound of the ocean inside of him. On your day, I stood at the end of the ocean and heard my brother's fistula in the ocean. It is the same sound, and standing there this was something that I knew for sure. With my heart, *par coeur*. It was a certainty that went beyond faith.

I described something in another letter by saying that I felt as though I have been emptied on this path. I thought of this again today and remembered with some wonder that on the first day my task was, in part, this:

> We let go of what is non-essential and embrace what is essential. We empty ourselves so that God may more fully work within us. And we become instruments in the hands of God.

I am still not sure about God, capital "G." But I can tell you that tonight at the ocean, having run for the sun and caught it, I felt completely and totally filled, from the earth up. Full yogic breath. Again. And Again.

I cannot believe that I am so blessed to have had this perfect magic follow me so far. The old man at Manjarin told both the Italian and me that Finisterre was the end, and it is.

Standing in the waves in twilight, I was so grateful for my tasks, for my friends, for my days, and for my own courage to dive into a softness that others might think silly and frivolous.

If I am not edgy, not tough enough – so what? For what? I have spent a lot of time on this Camino thinking, "For what?" That's not the right question. Life should be lived so that the question is "So what?"

So what that I've cried a bucket of tears this month? So what that I've had loss and pain and fear and whatever? I've been carrying that way too long. So what that I've written this all down and have said it out loud. So what if I'm going to die someday, no matter what I do? So what that I ran like a maniac? So what that I've lost my shoes? So what that I could go blind? So what that my daughter thinks I'm ridiculous?

Except there is a picture of her looking at me, when we found the sun, and in that moment, in that picture, I know that she does not think I am ridiculous at all. She gave me her shoes to walk back to town and she insisted on walking barefoot. My beautiful baby girl.

Malakai and I have a picture for you of us in the sunset. And what we made, dear Sue, was our footprints on a beach at the end of the world. With so much love, I could burst. Truly.

Love J.

25

N: I FEEL I AM missing so much of your life right now. George in Nepal and your pilgrimage in Spain. What spiritual awakening have you two been experiencing??! I have googled pilgrimage and the tasks but am unclear of the request (maybe because I have not yet read the google doc). What do you need from me? I will give it. I am just unclear what you want.

J. Just a task from you to me. That's all.

N. Your task from me: Give something away.

SANTIAGO, JULY 26, 2009

Dear Nancy:

I DID GIVE SOMETHING AWAY TODAY, but I can't tell you what it is. It was mine and mine alone. And it is now gone. Thank you.

I re-read our email exchange and laughed. Google is so great, but it does not answer everything! You googled pilgrimage and tasks, but this was not something that applied to me. I was not going on a pilgrimage. And I have no clue whether anyone else has ever taken tasks with them like this. Isn't that funny?

Anyone I talked to about this on the Camino was enthralled with the idea of my tasks. I agree that it was a good idea — but for me, it was only for me. I bristled when my new friends said one night at dinner, "So what is our task for tomorrow?" There is no "our," I thought. It's mine! My tasks are not a Camino accessory, they are mine! I have really only told the most surface of stories, nothing of the true meaning of what I have brought upon myself — except here in these letters. Had my new friends known the full fury of my daily tasks, perhaps they wouldn't have been so eager to want to share. I did indeed appreciate the encouragement, but I had to make sure I protected where I begin and end — something you know that I'm not particularly good at.

I am being unfair, of course, because my wonderful new friends immediately appreciated the thing that I have been quite afraid of: I called in my tribe, I asked, and I received. What a beautiful thing! And this is a story that perhaps I must share and give away. To view a tribe unconsciously at work in my life, in this way and in this place, is indeed enthralling. The piece of art that hangs in my front office says, in part, *to let the unbidden and the unconscious grow up through the common.* It is like that. I can see that. I know that.

Another friend said to me before I left that if she were doing this, she would do it this way, and that way, and another way. It felt a bit like judgment, and I hate being judged, but I know it wasn't intended that way. People use themselves always as a measuring stick against each other. This is what we do and it is one thing that I am consciously going to try to shed. I am not a measuring stick — for myself, or for anyone else. Whatever is in me is in me. What's mine is mine. That's it. Except that's not it. It runs deeper than that. Perhaps we always want to be each other, and simply forget all of the ways in which we are.

People say a lot of things about the Camino. But I didn't know. I didn't plan. I walked and I listened and I did what I was told. As I come close to the end now, on your day I know that I have remembered parts of myself that I had forgotten I had lost. I also did some long overdue grieving. I thought it would never end, but it did. On the fourth day, so long ago, I wrote to Ted that it was a day about walking through the pain to a point of thanksgiving. And, yesterday, I cried in thanksgiving to the ocean and deeply felt it a part of me.

On the train, on the way to the start of the Camino, I craved the openness and spontaneity and love that I saw among friends at the station in Paris. In the end, in Finisterre, I have thought about the last thirty days of mostly solitude and have felt more wrapped in love than I could have ever asked for. My tasks and my days have woven through so many coincidences and convergences, spontaneous and magical things that I cannot explain it fully. Malakai has told me to stop talking and write. She has also told me not to analyze things so much, so I have tried my best simply to observe, pay attention, and record the events and thoughts of each day in my letters. In doing so, I have laid myself bare — to myself, and now to you as you read this. It has brought me great pleasure and I think has given me a new way of using myself, or opening myself, in this world. If I am brave enough.

As for the question of giving something away: in concrete terms, I think it is more a question of what I have lost, because I keep losing things both intentionally and not. In Zubiri, I left a roll of toilet paper on purpose because it was too heavy. That may have also been where Malakai ditched the Spanish / English dictionary that would have come in quite handy. In Pamplona, when we arrived after the post office had closed, we left behind every little thing that we could. We rationed the clothes pegs. Somewhere before Portmarin, Malakai collected the laundry from the line and left my second shirt and my second pair of underwear behind. I was not happy about that.

I lost my Aveda lipstick somewhere, probably left on the edge of a sink. I left a squeeze bottle of laundry soap in Uterga. I then had to buy a bar of laundry soap, which I forgot in Finisterre. I lost Grace's Eco-Bag, which was a cause of great sadness because it was so strong and wonderful, like Grace. Both Malakai and I loved it, and it was the one thing that we fought about carrying — as in we both wanted to carry it. I have to find it online and replace it.

Malakai eventually lost her blue bandana and took mine. I have grown to love my bandana because it keeps my ears from burning and going all crusty like they did on the second day, so I will have to get it back from her. Although Malakai threw her Platypus across the floor at me one morning, it never did get left behind. I lost my toothbrush and went without for a full day. I also lost my lunch, as in woofed my cookies, on the bus to Finisterre. I did not like being on wheels.

I have not lost anything important, like my tasks or my special things that I am carrying, or my bits and pieces of paper with random scribbles and names and phone numbers. I have also not lost my Swiss army knife, my letters, or my beautiful, perfect socks.

I left my walking poles in Santiago somewhere — either at the pilgrimage office, the Cathedral, or the post office. I don't need them anymore, and now they are gone. I almost forgot them many, many times before — in bakeries, in bathrooms, or town squares — but they were too essential to lose them completely before now.

Yesterday, in Finisterre, I lost my sandals after catching the sun. The ocean, not surprisingly, took my shoes. I went back to get them and have somehow ended up in a photograph somewhere with a bunch of boisterous Spanish men. They tried to help me find them but my shoes were gone. Malakai quietly kicked hers off for me to wear and she walked barefoot all the way back to town.

I have a feeling that I have left a pile of other stuff that I won't remember or realize until I get home.

But what will I consciously give away after I return to my life? I don't know.

I started to shed several months ago when I decided that I couldn't keep up the pace much longer. There were days when I would wake with my file list in my mind as though my mind consisted only of a computer screen with lists of names and tasks. I was completely absent. I had checked myself out like a long-lost overdue library book, and I have moved from task to task, problem to problem, crisis to crisis, seamlessly, repeatedly, until I forgot what else my mind could do.

There were moments where from exhaustion, fear, or desperation I could not imagine living this way for twenty more years and prayed for total disability, death, divorce — anything to make it stop. I prayed for the things that I feared most, not what I wanted most, and not what I loved most. I prayed from and for a total denial of self. Autoimmune disease is exactly this. A denial by the self of the self. But it is beyond that. The body commits violence upon itself because it can no longer distinguish what is an external threat and what is an internal stressor. The body misfires, it moves out of step, and it attacks with all of its might. Once triggered, it is very difficult to bring things back in line. Each time I flare, it takes six months of steroid drops to bring my eyes under control. If that stops working, the other options are no fun.

To have the world go dark on one side is, for me, equal to a fear so powerful that I cannot express it. To have it linked to my brother's death, my sister's illness, and perhaps my mother's death is something I can barely consider.

THERE ARE OTHER THINGS I can barely consider. When I told Malakai the whole story, the full story, of Alexander, I realized that losing him was another "crisis" that received no time, no consideration. I know that in all of the grieving that I have done in the past month, I have still not caught up to him, my stillborn boy.

When I was labouring with him, I became scared because I had only had caesarean sections with Malakai and Mary. I didn't know what to expect or what to do. When we first arrived at the hospital, they me put me in a double room next to a woman who was simultaneously screaming and vomiting after losing her own baby. This was the late-term, dead-baby wing. It was hell. I tried to leave, in fact, but that was not an option.

After the poor woman beside me left, I was alone in the room with George for almost all of the night, except for the occasional nurse popping in to check on me. One nurse suggested that crying would not help, because "it" was going to come anyway. First of all, Alexander was not an "it" — even if he hadn't been named yet. Second, I never cry (or at least I never used to), so any idiot could see that I was suffering. I yelled at the nurse with such force that she didn't come back, ever.

But then no-one came, and we needed someone because I was scared.

Finally, they sent a young student nurse to deal with the bitch patient who was refusing to allow her dead baby to be called "it." The poor girl knew less of what to expect than I did. We were in the bathroom, all tiled white, and I was standing, hurting and scared. I did not want the silence that I knew was coming. The nurse, so young and full of care, dropped to the floor with a small basin and gently stroked my inner thigh while I cried and let him be born in all of his imperfect perfection. Poor beautiful boy. He had six toes on one foot, a cushion at the back of his neck where his brain had spilled, and a beautiful face. He had a big nose, which is no surprise.

Do you know that I barely said thank you to the friends and neighbours who cared for Stefan and Malakai and Kiki and Mary, for all of us during that time? My milk came in three days later, I wailed alone in the shower, and then a lost piece of placenta came out of me and fell onto the floor, producing screams that brought George tearing up the stairs.

That was it. We buried Alexander alone in the family cemetery. David Montgomery came to help us in his flowing Anglican robes and red Miata, and we carried on.

I have had many dark days here. But in walking I have allowed these things, too big to be contained only in me, to come up and out of me. I am emptied. You will see when you read my letters that I have been completely convinced of the magic of something larger than myself, and connected to me. I don't know what it is, beyond a feeling of light and vibration. I yearn for it and it for me, to the marrow of my spine; it moves me and moves in me. It is peace and it is grace and it is love. And it is here. Here. I am here. And I am thankful for the remainder of my life, in advance, and without reservation.

You have not missed any part of my life that was not worth missing, dear Nancy. You have always been there for the real stuff. Thank you for being an eternally patient friend.

Love J.

26

Hi Julie,

SO SORRY ABOUT THE DELAY on this. I have been trying
to think of something "good" for you, but have failed. Well, you
know me, and I am not going to let you pass up the opportunity
to be reflective. So, here's my task. While you are walking, reflect a bit on your life. For each decade of your life, think of five
things for that decade that were pivotal in defining who you are (I
was thinking about one thing per year, but none of our memories
are that good — are they?) Then, when you are done, think about
three things for each of the next five decades that you would like
to define your life. (I think you get the spirit of this. Feel free to
modify this to your own whimsy. Also, if everyone has given you
deep reflective tasks like this one, then feel free to just try to walk
the path for "my day" as straight as possible.)
Love, Garth

Dear Garth:

I WASN'T WALKING TODAY. THIS WAS the last day in Santiago and I am leaving tomorrow – first for Paris for one night and then home. While in Paris, I am going to take myself out for dinner in the most wonderful restaurant called Les Fêtes Galantes. I will have to send you the address so that you can go there while you are in France on sabbatical.

How did we get so grown up, anyway? Sabbaticals and dinner in Paris. . . .

I have some math questions for you, which I have been saving up. But now, as I write, I think it would take too long to explain them in one letter. I'll have to send you all of my letters, and you will then see all of the times when I have placed a thought in reserve for you. "I'll have to ask Garth, the math genius of great faith." We will need to see each other and talk at some length to continue the discussion that you and I very clearly started when we were fifteen. That conversation is not done.

I woke up this morning, on the last day of this pilgrimage of mine, and read your task. What is wonderful about it is that I can respond to you in shorthand at the end of this long journey and you will know exactly what I mean.

In response to your task, I wrote down a quick summary of life to date so I could continue to ponder it throughout the day before coming to rest on the specifics. This is what I came up with:

0-10	Love of my mother
11-20	Death of my mother. Confusion of self / non-self
21-30	Non-self
31-40	Work & Illness

The last two decades don't look very fun when I write it like that. That's not true. It's just been too busy for very many clear moments of pure, uncluttered joy. Life can get like that. Life gets in the way.

Malakai and I chatted the afternoon away, happily nestled on comfy chairs in a restaurant that we found near the cathedral. It was a day that was more or less full of ease.

At the end of the day, very late, I had not finished your task. I was stuck on 0-10. I remember significant things from when I was four and five, but not so much after that. The years from six to ten felt completely blank, and trying to remember was making my brain hurt. I didn't want to skip ahead, so I put it aside and packed and puttered away the day.

Close to midnight, I was at a computer place around the corner from the hotel, on Facebook with George, giving him flight details, telling him that I loved him, wanting to be home. He was absent for a while on the computer and then came back to tell me that he had been on the phone with a woman named Patty Turner who had called me from Kentucky, looking for my dad.

An absolute flood of memories returned to me as I sat, amazed, on the stool in front of that computer in the little cubicle. Patty Turner gave me a white ceramic painted poodle that held my childhood door open. You would have seen it, I'm sure, at the house on Cherry Lane, but you wouldn't remember it.

Patty was my mother's very dear friend when I was very young, from about age six to nine, until they moved back to Kentucky. Patty was present, I am now thinking, for most of the conscious period of my childhood before my mother got sick. I remember them at the house on Clarkson, actually, so it would have been even earlier than that. I was four when we lived on Clarkson.

I remember Patty clearly at our house on Cherry Lane, and at the Rosslyn Village mobile home park where they lived and where my brother also lived. That was close to your house, wasn't it? I've never had any sense of direction — you know that. But I think your parents' house was out that way. I can't believe I can't remember.

I used to stand at the living-room picture window waiting for Patty and Jonathan to pull into the driveway. I would jump up and down yelling "Patty's home! Patty's home!" in great joy because I loved her. George said that this is exactly what Patty told him too.

Patty was beautiful and she had a beautiful voice, and as I sat on Facebook typing all of this to George, I could see Patty and my mother in the kitchen. My mother was beautiful and had a beautiful voice too, and it made me so happy to be able to see her. I could hear my mother's voice laughing — a sound I have not heard, or been able to remember, for almost exactly thirty years. She got sick on August 10, 1979, and I haven't been able to return to the memory of her singing or the memory of her laughter since then.

I have not spoken to Patty Turner for longer than that. I tried to call her tonight but it wouldn't work. That is something that is waiting for me to do when I get home.

How very, very strange to have such a wonderful thing happen on my last day, just before midnight. Can you believe it? Of course you can, because you have faith.

And so onto your task. I'm not stumped anymore.

0-10:

1. There is a video of me dancing in the living room, ecstatic. My mother was always taking the video so there are very few videos of her, except when they were in Bermuda where I was conceived. I was a happy child and I was loved.

2. My mother was always in the kitchen peeling potatoes or in her room sewing things, including tiny satin or polyester Barbie-doll clothes for me. She laughed about things and she loved tomatoes.

3. My dad bought me strawberries and tried to get me not to be afraid of worms in the garden. We made a popsicle stick fruit basket in the basement.

4. My sisters and my brother were much older and were busy getting married and having babies. The house was always full and my mother was always there. We made Kleenex flowers for all of the cars for all of the weddings.

5. I climbed the poplar trees in the backyard and burned out the headlines of the newspaper with a magnifying glass on the front step. I was not afraid.

11-20

1. My mother got sick. She stayed sick. And then she died. Does that count as one thing or three things?

2. You and I met, and started going to the youth-group stuff in Winnipeg. The formative things in my life mirrored yours in those years, didn't they?

3. Canada World Youth at age seventeen.

4. Trent University at age eighteen. Are you older or younger than me? I can never remember. Your Trent friends didn't

like me, ever. Why was that? Anyway, by the time I was twenty, you were gone – off to be a math genius.

5. I stopped asking the big questions because they were becoming too difficult.

21-30

1. I married Malakai's dad.

2. Malakai was born.

3. Her dad left.

4. I fell in love with George (and Stefan and Kiki).

5. I finished my Master's Degree.

6. I went to law school.

7. We moved to Millbrook.

8. George's dad died.

9. Mary was born.

10. We lost Alexander. You and Catherine were at our house for lunch the day I had the ultrasound, but we never really talked about it after that. I think that's the only time you've been to the house. Am I right? You couldn't come to the wedding.

That's ten. A heavy decade with nothing that I could leave out of the "pivotal" category.

31-40

1. George and I got married.

2. I was called to the Bar and started practising law.

3. Marty died.

4. My brother got sick.

5. George got sick.

6. My dad got sick.

7. I got sick.

8. My brother died.

9. My sisters got sick.

10. The kids grew.

That's ten again, all pivotal. And #11 would be that I am here, a tired pilgrim.

As for the next five decades, I have decided to keep it very, very simple:

41-50: Finish growing the kids. Pay everything off. Travel.
51-60: Read. Write. Be Quiet.
61-70: Grow my garden. Walk like Barbara. Make young friends.
71-80: Grow wise. Be graceful. Become like Grace.
81-90: Approach death. Welcome death. Have faith.

Maybe somewhere in there I'll come to understand math, though I doubt it. But what I can say to you – my dear friend with the rational, mathematical mind, whose faith has always been so strong and sure – is that I know the universal truth is light and love and I know that it perfectly matches a light and a lightness deep within me. I have decided to throw off the cynical and pessimistic world that I have created around myself and love my life, as the true spark of light that it is.

Paso por paso. Step by step. I have my proof.

Onward...

Love J.

Afterword

Dear Malakai:

TODAY IS MY MOTHER'S BIRTHDAY. She would have turned eighty. Yesterday was the anniversary of her death and I thought of her grave-plaque, where the deer did his business, with my father's body now tucked in beneath and to her left. All of the dates on the grave-plaque are now filled in.

Just after Grandpa died, and just before Christmas, you asked me whether I had any regrets about walking the Camino. You asked this because you thought that perhaps our walk led to the implosion we each experienced at the close of the year.

I have thought about this a lot since then. No, I have no regrets but neither did I expect what has followed. After the Camino, I thought it was just a matter of integration. I thought I could fit myself back into my life. And I thought you could and would do the same. You are young. Suck it up. Carry on. And for God's sake, don't cry. Do as your mother taught you. That's part of it, isn't it? You know that. But there is another lesson. Another way.

When I went to see Proud Woman in August, with my beautiful hawk in hand, I received many, many gifts — none of which I yet understand. One of the things she gave me was an eagle feather which is a sacred thing, a holy thing, and a gift that requires things of me that I do not yet know.

First comes the medicine, then the journey.

Sometimes, it would appear, the journey takes you to the very edge of a precipice and you are forced to claw your way back in the dark. Sometimes it takes you to the place of your greatest fear.

In the weeks before Grandpa died, when all around me spun into chaos, I was in that place. In sitting with him, and sleeping with him, as he prepared to die, I was forced to sit with my own fear, and my own pain, and my own darkness. Day after day, night after night, as death was watching, wrapping me in its black smell.

Of course, Grandpa kept joking and telling stories to the end and some of those last days were ridiculously funny. As his circulation moved to the centre of him, and his toes turned black from the diabetes — first wet and seeping, then virtually mummified — he stuck his toes high in the air and told me to remember that death starts in feet. We laughed, and I watched and waited as the black crept higher and he started to leave this world. Perhaps it was the palliative drugs that did it, but there were many times that he stopped breathing for far too long, then revived with tears and awe to tell me about the places he had been soaring to, far beyond the orbit of the earth. That is what he said. He said it was beautiful there.

I read my letters to my dad, by the way. We were going to send them to the printer on November 11th, which is the day that he started to die. In the morning, George told me that we should wait until the end of that week to send the letters off because I should read them out loud to catch the last mistakes. Shortly after George said that, the phone rang and it was Grandpa's nurse to tell me to come. I brought the letters with me and read them out loud to Grandpa twice before he died. I know that he was listening because he laughed a lot – especially at the parts about my mother's morning mood, the Cow Palace milk jug, Betty Ilkew's sheets across the back fence, stolen raspberries, water fights, and children hanging in the poplar trees.

I also brought my things to him: my hawk wings, my claw, my eagle feather, my snails, my flute. I showed them to Grandpa only once. For some strange reason this happened when Patrick the undertaker was there to help us with funeral arrangements. As Patrick sat watching in his pristine black coat, I played show and tell with my dad. Grandpa held up my bear claw and told me about the ancient Celtic symbol in the moon and star of my claw and bell (for this is how it is strung, perfectly oriented to my body as Glenn said). My dad also told me that when I was a small girl I collected things – some of which only I could see – and brought them to him in my cupped hands. He told me not to hide from myself. Daddy, can you see me?

Patrick was also there when I tucked a small snail shell into Grandpa's cupped hands, before his body was shipped north to my sisters. I had to move his pinky finger to do this and I was not afraid.

My dad asked me one day through the pain to tell him what was happening to him. I didn't know what to say. I told him I thought it was a bit like being a butterfly trying to get out of the cocoon and it was the hardest work we will ever have to do. He cried from the pain and from the approach of death. Later, in the middle of the night, he was in the bathroom with one of his caregivers and he shouted out to me from the bathroom: "What were you saying about the cocoon?" I repeated what I had said and his response was, very quietly, this: "Not very many people are ever able to break free from their cocoon."

Right to the end, Grandpa loved music. You saw the way he was, conducting a full orchestra from his bed. Kiki and Mary danced in his room to Johnny Cash a couple of days before he died, after he had stopped talking. I can still see the joy in his eyes and the love in his face all through that day without words. It was pure. Uncluttered. Unlocked. Like a dog's face.

One afternoon, Grandpa was holding his violin bow in his hand while music was playing and he was talking about Ford Rupert again, which made me cry. As the sun shone into his room, I put my head down on the side of his bed because I was so tired and so sad. My dad took his violin bow, moving in time to the music, and softly bowed my hair as I sobbed into his mattress. That was the day I really learned how to cry. We are frozen music.

So cry, dear girl. Scream. Break free. Take heart and gather your courage. Feed your soul. Don't walk in the shadows. Don't fret about all of the people. Fly. Fly. Fly.

There is a light and a lightness in you that longs to dance with the power of the whole universe. Throw off the pessimistic world that lives around you and love yourself for the pure spirit of light that you are.

Love, Mommy.